Indian Cooking

with

FOUR INGREDIENTS

Quick, easy, every day, authentic Indian
recipes using only four ingredients

Jasprit Bhangal

Matador
9 Priory Business Park
Kibworth Beauchamp
Leicestershire LE8 0RX, UK
Tel: (+44) 116 279 2299
Fax: (+44) 116 279 2277
Email: books@troubador.co.uk
Web: www.troubador.co.uk/matador

ISBN 978 1780884 868

British Library Cataloguing in Publication Data.
A catalogue record for this book is available from the British Library.

Typeset in 11pt Adobe Garamond Pro by Troubador Publishing Ltd, Leicester, UK

Matador is an imprint of Troubador Publishing Ltd

Photo Credits- Cover front and back

GJ Singh
Indyum
www.indiyum.com.au

www.indiancookingfouringredients.com

Printed and bound in the UK by TJ International, Padstow, Cornwall

To:

My daughter
Navneet Bhangal

And

My son
Navtej Bhangal

I hope you find this book useful and a reminder of home cooked Indian food and that it will help you in creating your very own creations.

Contents

Foreword

Growing up in England, but being born in India, Indian cuisine has always been a part of my life. I was taught cooking by my mother, who was taught by her own mother. I hope I've also inherited some of her formidable cooking expertise. Within a remarkably short space of time, my mother is able to get two to three main meals ready along with raita, salad, chutney, chapati and a sweet.

Just like in my family, Indian recipes are orally passed down through the generations, from mothers to daughters and daughter-in-laws. It is only relatively recently that recipes have been written down. My mother did not receive written recipes from my grandmother, who was an incredible cook, so I write down recipes from my mother in the hope that one day I can pass these on, not only to my own children but to a wider audience.

Needless to say, I'm passionate about Indian cookery. However, I also encounter plenty of misconceptions. A common perception of Indian cuisine is that it is mainly comprised of curries and yet 'curry' is not even an Indian word. There is so much more to Indian cooking than what people usually encounter in restaurants and takeaways. However, when I encourage people to try cooking Indian food at home for themselves, I often hear a number of objections and concerns. The reasons for not cooking Indian are many and varied:

It involves too many ingredients
It is too difficult
It is too complicated
The food is too hot or spicy
People don't know where to begin
They don't have the time

Yet Indian cooking doesn't have to be any of the above. I have tried to dispel various myths about Indian cooking in this book. By reducing the number of ingredients, my mission is to make Indian food easy and accessible. I want to prove that anyone can create wonderful Indian dishes in their own home in a short amount of time with little fuss. The recipes in this book include many well-known curries, but also simple dishes which can be whipped up in a matter of minutes.

There is no real reason to be intimidated by Indian cuisine. Getting Indian food to taste wonderful is not necessarily about having the exact ingredients and following a strict recipe. It is more about adding spices to fresh ingredients according to your own individual taste. I hope to encourage you to experiment, as Indian cuisine is best approached in the spirit of improvisation. You will have probably noticed that if you have tasted a particular dish in one Indian establishment and order the same dish in another, the meal will not taste exactly the same. Often, even if you go back to the same place, it will taste slightly different. This is because Indian cooks do not generally use measures but make estimates. Cooks at home will add ingredients according to what is available to them. I want to encourage you to adopt this relaxed and creative approach too.

At the core of my approach is simplicity. Our busy contemporary lifestyles often involve balancing the demands of careers with family, and so little time is left for cooking. I have created recipes which are easy and can be prepared quickly, without compromising on taste. These recipes were put to the ultimate test by my daughter and son when they left home for university. They were always calling and asking for Indian recipes. Being on a budget and not having much time, they were looking for easy recipes that they could make quickly. They invariably went down a treat.

The idea for this book came about when I was on a visit to Australia. I was often asked for Indian recipes by my Australian friends, especially Maurice Forde, Helen Watson and Derek Watson. When I served them my dishes, I often received comments such as 'Gosh, it must have taken all day'. In fact the reality of most of the dishes was that they were prepared quickly. We enjoyed many barbeques, lunches, picnics and dinners that were put together in a matter of minutes.

With the encouragement and help of Helen Watson, we soon pulled together my recipes in order to create this book. Helen Watson has been instrumental in the making of this collection; both in helping me collate and test the recipes. Her hard work and support has been the most special ingredient I've used in creating this book. We both hope that you too will enjoy the recipes. Try them and see for yourself, we know that you will not be disappointed.

History of Indian Cuisine

India is predominantly vegetarian due to religious and cultural beliefs, but meat is eaten by many and this is normally based on family or personal preferences. Beef is banned in India and only available in the state of Goa. The Hindu religion prohibits its followers from eating beef and the cow is regarded as scared because it ploughs our fields, to harvest food and provides us with milk. Goa has a large community of Catholics and Christians. In fact, the type of foods eaten is closely allied to religious practice in India. For example, the Muslim population do not eat pork, not only in India but around the world.

To add to this complex picture, the different regions in India have their own unique dishes and use of spices. What is important to note is that each region will use locally-sourced fresh ingredients and add spice to make their own unique style of dish. For example, the Punjab region is known for its agricultural production of dairy and wheat. Therefore dishes such as paneer and saag originate from there. Fish is widely available near the coastal regions of India; therefore fish dishes are popular there.

Moreover, Indian cuisine is far from a static body of knowledge. Indian cookery dates back many centuries and has evolved over time, thanks to the many influences brought by invasions and conquests. One of the most important influences was the Mogul rule, which had a major influence on Indian food and the style of cooking. The Moguls were renowned for their big banquets with rich foods and this is where recipes with cream, nuts and dried fruits have evolved. From when the Portuguese arrived in India to trade in spices, they left their own stamp on Indian cuisine, introducing vinegar into meat dishes. The most well-known is vindaloo which is derived from the Portuguese dish "Carne de Vinha d'Alhos", a dish of meat, usually pork, with wine and garlic from the time the Portuguese were in India.

During the heyday of the British Empire, India was known as 'The Brightest Jewel in the Crown' due to its many natural riches such as diamonds, cotton, wheat and spices. While the British were in India, they adapted many dishes for their own taste, recipes for Worcestershire sauce, mulligatawny soup, and kedgeree to name a few. After India obtained its independence, the British love of Indian food stayed with the people who had lived in India during the time of occupation, but not to the extent that it is today.

The first Indian restaurant was opened in England in 1810 by an Indian soldier, who followed his friend to England from the East India company. He was called Sake Dean Mahomed and was born a Muslim in Patna, India, but later on converted to Anglican denomination of Christianity. The restaurant was called the Hindoostane Coffee House and was located at 34 George Street, off Portman Square in London. The restaurant did not actually serve coffee. However, it was noted to be a place where the nobility and gentry could enjoy Indian dishes of the highest quality.

Unfortunately, the restaurant did not do well, and it was forced into bankruptcy in 1812. Dean Mahomed had wanted to appeal to the British people who had returned from India. However, people generally did not go out to eat in restaurants as they had chefs at home to cook for them. The premises are now a building called Carlton House.

Indian restaurants have come a long way from the days of the Hindoostane Coffee House. Today, they have proliferated into every corner of the United Kingdom. Several years ago, chicken tikka masala replaced fish and chips as Britain's favourite national dish.

Hindoostane Coffee House

However, whilst there is so much more to Indian food and cooking than chicken tikka masala, exploring a wider range of Indian cuisine need not be difficult. Indian food is adapting to its new British environment, particularly our busy contemporary lifestyles. In this cookbook, I want to show how you can enjoy new kinds of Indian food without too much stress.

Indian Cuisine in the UK – Facts and Figures

- Indian food has become the largest food industry in the UK.

- The Indian food industry in the UK is worth £4.2 billion and accounts for two-thirds of all eating out.

- There are about 12,000 Indian curry houses in the UK, employing an estimated 70,000 staff.

- Chicken tikka masala is the UK's most popular dish. It originated in Britain.

- Britons spend more than £5 million a day in Indian restaurants.

- Indian restaurants in Britain serve more than 1 million customers every day.

- In London, there are more Indian restaurants than in Mumbai and Delhi.

- Supermarkets sell 1.5 million packets of chicken tikka masala every year.

- Each year the UK eats enough papadums to circle the world.

- Indian restaurants in UK use more than 200,000 tonnes of rice a year.

- 19 tons of chicken tikka masala is sold by department store Marks & Spencer in their food department every week.

- Supermarket Sainsbury's sells over one million portions of chicken tikka masala every year.

- One in seven curries sold in Indian curry houses is chicken tikka masala.

Introduction to the Four Ingredients Method

In this cookbook I have not included the following ingredients as part of the recipes although they may be needed to make the dish:

- Water, as this is part of the process in recipes rather than an ingredient.

- Seasoning of salt and chilli flakes. Since the introduction of chilli into Pepper is not normally used in Indian cooking. I don't normally use pepper and only use chilli flakes or chilli powder. Use as little or as much chilli as you like to suit your taste.

- Cooking oil, since it is a cooking method rather than an ingredient. Most cooking in India is performed using ghee, but we have used olive oil in this book since it is more readily available and the end result is just as good. Vegetable oil can also be used. Spices need to be cooked in oil to release their aroma and flavour.

- In the Curries section, I have used the base ingredients for a curry and then added four ingredients to complete the dish. These basic ingredients of Indian curries include the essentials of onions, ginger and garlic, as stated by the UK Food Standards Agency.

- In the Dhal / Lentil section, I have shown the recipe for the dhal and then used four ingredients for the tarka. In a dhal, the lentils are boiled to soften them and then, just before serving, a tempering of tarka is added. This tarka is what makes the dhals taste wonderful and why dhals are often listed on menus as tarka dhal.

- In the Saag section, I have shown the recipe for saag, followed by the tarka recipe. As with the dhal, a tempering of tarka is applied to the portion of saag being served. For these recipes, I have used butter since butter is what makes the dish taste so good.

- Coriander leaves are often used as garnish, when not included as an ingredient.

Before we proceed, do bear a couple of principles in mind. In Indian cooking, meat is always fully cooked, and should not be pink or red in the middle.

Also, all curry pastes should be gently but thoroughly cooked as this releases the flavour of their spices.

Abbreviations, Oven Temperatures and Measurements

To make the following recipes really easy, I have used the following abbreviations, oven temperatures and measurements.

Abbreviations Used

Gram	g
Kilogram	kg
Millilitre	ml
Litre	ltre
Teaspoon	tsp
Tablespoon	tbsp

Oven Temperature

Fahrenheit	350°F
Celsius	180°C
Gas Mark	4

Measurements

Cup	250ml
1 Teaspoon	5ml
1 Tablespoon	15ml

Essential Indian Spices and Grocery Items

There are a number of essential spices and grocery items that are staples in an Indian kitchen. Having a good supply of these items in your pantry will save you time and money. The spices should be stored in airtight containers and away from direct sunlight. This will ensure that they remain fresh for longer.

Below is a list of recommended essential spices and grocery items. Not all will necessarily be required, but choose the ones that you will use again and again. The Indian spices can be purchased from good Indian grocery stores, although plenty of supermarkets now stock a good range of them too.

Basmati rice	Rice is a good accompaniment to Indian cooking and basmati rice is a particularly authentic choice
Chapati flour (atta)	A type of flour used to make Indian Breads
Oil	Olive oil is a good choice. Spices need to be cooked in oil and nearly all recipes need oil at some stage
Tinned tomatoes, with or without garlic	Add to make curries
Tinned chickpeas	Quick and easy to make a high protein and low-fat curry
Red lentils (dhal)	Extremely simple to cook
Lemon juice	Used as flavour

Cumin seeds and Cumin Powder	Used in many recipes
Garam masala	A spice blend added to many recipes, either in cooking or it can be just sprinkled over the top of food just before serving
Curry paste	Handy item for quick curries
Curry powder	Used in some recipes
Garlic and ginger paste	Handy item often used in curries
Butter	Especially good for spreading over breads
Chilli flakes	Use as much or as little to taste
Chaat Masala	Used to impart a sweet sour flavour

Snacks
and
Starters

Indian cuisine is full of flavor and is evolving and adapting all the time, some of these recipe names may not appear to be Indian but they are just as authentic and create wonderful meals for you to enjoy and share with family and friends.

As a child I remember enjoying sweet eggy bread for breakfast which my Mum used to make, because this was the only way I would eat eggs. This recipe was passed to my mother from my grandmother.

Breakfast

Breakfast in India varies from region to region, but it is always wholesome, prepared with great care and with fresh, seasonal ingredients.

Fresh fruit and yoghurt feature in most regions, as do eggs scrambled with tomatoes and spices.

South India is famous for dosas, similar to crepes or pancakes, and typically folded over and filled with spiced potatoes, coconut and or lentils. Idli are steamed cakes made with fermented rice and lentils.

North Indian breakfast often consists of parathas and leavened breads, often with a variety of fillings including potatoes, vegetables and lentils, and served with yoghurt and or chutneys.

Another breakfast dish from northern India is khichri which is usually made with rice and lentils. During the colonial era in India, the English adapted the kitchri dish by adding smoked haddock, cream and eggs. They renamed it 'kedgeree', according to their phonetic translation of the original.

Lunch

Lunch in India again varies from region to region. It is invariably a light meal and often consists of a dhal, vegetable or spicy meat dish, accompanied by rice and/or chapati with chutney. Often people who work away from home will take their lunches in a container called a 'Tiffin', hence the origin of the phrase 'Tiffin lunch'.

In Mumbai, there are Tiffin Wallahs who deliver lunch in Tiffin boxes to hundreds of people working in offices. In the UK and the US, a Tiffin lunch has recently become popular, with many people bringing home-cooked lunches to their offices in a Tiffin box, very similar to the lunch box.

Indian Omelette
Serves 2

4 eggs
½ onion, finely diced
½ tsp garam masala
Handful chopped fresh coriander

In a bowl beat the eggs with the chopped onion, garam masala and coriander, season with salt and chilli flakes. Heat a lightly greased frying pan, add the egg mixture and swirl around so that the base is covered with the mixture. Cook on a low heat until the bottom is cooked. Flip the omelette over and cook the other side. Remove onto a plate and fold in half.

Serve with parathas.

Omelette Meal
Serves 2

4 eggs
½ onion, finely chopped
2 tomatoes, finely diced
1 green pepper, finely chopped

In a bowl, beat the eggs with the onions, tomatoes, green pepper, and season with salt and chilli flakes to taste. Heat a little oil in a small frying pan and pour the mixture into the pan, and swirl around so that the egg mixture covers the bottom of the frying pan. Cook gently until there is no liquid and the bottom starts to turn brown. Turn the omelette over and cook the other side until cooked through. Remove from heat, on to a plate and fold in half.

Serve with parathas.

Indian Scrambled Eggs
Serves 2

4 eggs
2 whole green chillies, finely chopped
½ onion, finely chopped
2 tbsp butter

In a bowl, beat the eggs with the chopped green chillies and onion, season with salt. Heat the butter in a frying pan and pour the egg mixture into the frying pan, stirring using a wooden spoon. Keep stirring until the eggs are cooked through and not runny.

Serve with parathas.

Eggy Bread
Serves 2

4 eggs
4 slices of bread cut into triangles
½ tsp garam masala

In a bowl, beat the eggs with garam masala and season with salt and chilli flakes to taste. Heat a little oil in a frying pan. Dip the bread triangles into the egg mixture and place into the heated pan. Cook until one side turns a golden brown colour, flip over and cook the other side.

Serve.

Sweet Eggy Bread
Serves 2

4 eggs
3 tbsp of sugar
4 slices of bread cut into triangles

Heat a frying pan with a little oil. In a bowl, beat the eggs with the sugar. Dip the bread triangles into the egg mixtures and place into the frying pan. Cook until one side turns a golden brown colour, then flip over and cook the other side.

Serve.

Eggy Bread with Cinnamon
Serves 2

4 eggs
4 slices of bread, cut into quarters
2 tsp cinnamon sugar
½ cup milk

Heat a frying pan with 1 tbsp oil. Mix together the eggs and cinnamon sugar with milk. Dip the bread quarters into the mixture and let it soak for a few minutes. Add the coated bread to the frying pan and brown on one side, then turn over and brown the other side.

Serve with fresh fruit.

Tomatoes on Toast
Serves 2

4 bread slices
4 tomatoes, sliced
4 tsp mango chutney

Toast the bread and cut in half, removing the crusts if you prefer. Spread mango chutney over the toast then arrange tomato slices on top of the chutney, season with salt and drizzle with a little oil. Place under a grill and cook until the tomatoes have browned.

Serve alone or with an omelette.

Fruit Salad
Serves 2

A mixture of fresh cut fruit, including apples, bananas, oranges, etc.
2 tsp chaat masala

Place the fruit into a bowl and sprinkle the chaat masala over the top. Toss to combine.

Serve.

Tomato and Chilli Penne Pasta
Serves 2

2 cups penne pasta
1 jar of tomato and chilli pasta sauce
1 tsp cumin seeds
2 tbsp lemon juice

In a saucepan, add penne pasta and cook with water to packet instructions. In a frying pan add the cumin seeds to a little oil and fry for about 1 minute. Add the pasta sauce, season with salt and chilli flakes and add ½ cup water. Bring to the boil, lower heat and simmer until the water has evaporated. Add the cooked penne pasta to the saucepan and stir to combine. Just before serving add the lemon juice.

Serve.

Bread Pakoras
Serves 2

4 white bread slices
1 cup besan (chickpea flour)
2 tsp mango powder
½ tsp garam masala

Cut the crusts off the slices of bread and cut into 4 triangles, then keep aside. In a bowl, combine the besan, mango powder and garam masala, season with salt and chilli flakes. Adding water slowly, 1 tbsp at a time, make a batter, mixing at the same time to avoid lumps forming. In a frying pan heat some oil for deep frying. Dip the bread pieces into the batter mixture until they are coated both sides. Drop the coated bread pieces into the frying pan and deep fry until golden brown. Remove onto kitchen paper to drain.

Serve with tamarind chutney for dipping.

Potato Pakoras

Serves 2

2 potatoes cut into rounds
1 cup besan (chickpea Flour)
2 tsp pomegranate powder
1 tsp garam masala

In a bowl, combine besan, pomegranate powder and garam masala, season with salt and chilli flakes. Adding water slowly make a thick batter, mixing at the same time to avoid lumps forming. Heat some oil in a frying pan for deep frying. Add the potato rounds to the batter and mix to coat. Drop the coated potato rounds into the oil and deep fry until golden brown. Remove onto kitchen paper to drain.

Serve with a chutney of your choice.

Onion Pakoras

Serves 2

1 onion, cut into rounds
1 cup besan (chickpea flour)
1 tsp mango powder
1 tsp garam masala

In a bowl, combine besan, mango powder and garam masala, season with salt and chilli flakes. Adding water slowly make a thick batter, mixing at the same time, to avoid lumps forming. Heat some oil in a frying pan for deep frying. Add the onion circles into the batter and mix to coat. Drop the onion rings into the oil and deep fry until golden brown. Remove onto kitchen paper to drain.

Serve with a chutney of your choice.

Vegetable Samosas
Serves 4

Cold cooked cumin potatoes (see page 81)
4 sheets filo pastry

Cut the sheets of filo pastry into 3 long strips, making sure to cover the remaining filo pastry not being used with a damp tea towel to prevent it from drying out. Place 1 tbsp of cumin potatoes into one corner and fold the pastry diagonally and keep folding until the pastry is used up. Use a little oil to seal the ends. Spray or brush the samosas with oil. Place the samosas onto a greased baking tray and bake in the oven at 180°C for 30 minutes until golden brown. Turn over once during cooking.

Serve with tamarind chutney or a chutney of your choice.

Meat Samosas
Serves 4

Cold cooked mince curry (see page 51)
4 sheets filo pastry

Cut the sheets of filo pastry into 3 long strips, making sure to cover the remaining filo pastry not being used with a damp tea towel to prevent it from drying out. Place 1 tbsp of the mince curry into one corner and fold the pastry diagonally and keep folding until the pastry is used up. Use a little oil to seal the ends. Spray or brush the samosas with oil. Place the samosas on to a greased baking tray and bake in the oven at 180°C for 30 minutes until golden brown. Turn over once during cooking.

Serve with tamarind chutney or a chutney of your choice.

Masala Peanuts
Serves 6

1 cup unsalted peanuts
1 cup besan (chickpea flour)
2 tsp mango powder

In a bowl, mix the besan with mango powder and season with salt and chilli flakes. Add the peanuts and stir in water, one tablespoon at a time, and keep stirring. The peanuts should be covered with the flour, and try not to make the batter too thin. It should be fairly stiff and stick to the peanuts. If there are dry bits of flour that is fine too as long as the peanuts are covered with the besan mixture. Heat oil in a frying pan and carefully drop the peanuts into the oil. If the peanuts stick together in the pan separate gently. Fry until golden brown and drain on kitchen paper.

Serve.

Paneer Tikka
Serves 4

200g paneer, cut into large cubes (see page 80)
2 tbsp tandoori tikka paste
2 tbsp plain yoghurt
2 tsp mango powder

In a bowl, mix the tandoori paste and yoghurt with mango powder, season with salt and chilli flakes. Add the paneer pieces and mix to coat them. Leave to marinade for 1 hour. Grill or barbecue the paneer tikka, turning once to ensure both sides are cooked.

Serve with a chutney of your choice.

Cod and Chutney
Serves 2

4 pieces of cod, cut into 2 inch pieces
1 tbsp lemon juice
1 tbsp mango chutney

In a bowl, mix the chutney with lemon juice and season with salt and chilli flakes. Add the fish and mix to coat. Cover and leave for 1 hour to marinate. Place the fish onto a greased baking tray and bake in the oven for 30 minutes at 180°C degrees or until cooked, turning over once.

Serve.

Aloo and Paneer Chaat
Serves 2

100g paneer cut into cubes see page 80
1 potato, cut into small cubes
2 tsp mango powder
1 tsp cumin powder

In a frying pan, heat 2 tbsp of oil. Add the paneer cubes and gently fry until they have turned brown in colour. Once they have browned add the potato cubes and cumin powder to the frying pan, season with salt and chilli flakes, and add ¼ cup water, bring to boil. Lower heat and cook until the potatoes are tender and the water has evaporated, stir often to prevent the mixture sticking to the pan. Sprinkle the mango powder into the pan and stir to mix. Remove onto a plate.

Serve with tamarind chutney.

Buttermilk Onion Rings

Serves 4

1 cup buttermilk
½ cup flour
1 onion, cut into rings
2 tbsp chaat masala

In a bowl, season the flour with salt and chilli flakes. Add the buttermilk and combine to form a batter, ensuring no lumps form. Add the onions and coat in the batter. Heat oil in a frying pan and add the onions rings to the oil and fry until they are golden brown. Remove onto kitchen paper to drain. Sprinkle chaat masala over the top before serving.

Serve.

Mince and Onion Tarts

Serves 4

2 sheets ready-made puff pastry
1 cup cooked mince curry see page 51
½ onion, finely chopped
1 tbsp fresh coriander, chopped

Cut the pastry sheets into 8 pieces. Place onto a baking tray and fold edges to make a crust. Prick the pastry with a fork. Bake in the oven at 180°C for 10 minutes. Remove from oven. Place a spoonful of the mince curry over the pastry and sprinkle with onion, and then sprinkle with chopped coriander. Place back in the oven and bake for another 10 minutes.

Serve.

Tangy Chips
Serves 4

4 potatoes, cut into thin rounds
2 tsp mango powder
1 tsp cumin powder

Heat oil in a frying pan and fry the potatoes until they are crispy; if you double fry, by simply removing from pan and leave to stand for a few minutes, and then fry again, the chips become even crispier. Remove onto kitchen paper to drain. In a bowl, mix salt and chilli flakes with mango powder and cumin powder. Toss the chips in this mixture.

Serve.

Spicy Popcorn
Serves 4

1 cup popping corn
2 tsp mango powder

Pop the corn in a pan with a lid with 2 tbsp of oil. When the popping stops, the corn is done. Remove into a bowl, and sprinkle a little salt and chilli flakes and mango powder over the popcorn and toss to distribute the seasoning evenly.

Serve.

Potato and Coriander Chaat
Serves 4

4 boiled potatoes, diced
1 cup coriander chutney
2 tsp chaat masala

Season the potatoes with salt and chilli flakes. In a frying pan add 1 tbsp of oil and fry the potatoes until golden brown in colour. Remove from the pan and place onto a plate to cool. When cooled, pour the coriander chutney over the potatoes and mix together. Sprinkle chaat masala over the top.

Serve.

Stuffed Sweet Peppers
Serves 2

2 large sweet peppers
4 oz cream cheese
½ tsp garam masala
½ tsp coriander powder

In a bowl, mix the cream cheese with the coriander powder and garam masala, season with salt and chilli flakes. Keep aside. Cut the tops of the jalapeño peppers and remove the seeds. Fill the peppers with the cream cheese mixture and brush with oil. Place onto a greased baking tray and bake for 25 minutes at 180°C or until they are cooked.

Serve.

Prawn Pakoras
Serves 4

500g prawns
½ cup rice flour
1 tsp curry powder
1 cup besan (chickpea flour)

In a bowl, add the besan, rice flour and curry powder, season with salt and chilli flakes. Stir in water gradually until a very thick batter is formed, ensuring no lumps are formed. Add the prawns to the batter and mix to coat. Heat some oil in a pan for deep frying and fry the coated prawns in oil until golden brown. Remove to kitchen paper to drain.

Serve with a chutney of your choice.

Prawns in Breadcrumbs
Serves 4

500g prawns
2 tbsp curry paste
½ cup yoghurt
2 cups breadcrumbs

In a bowl, add the curry paste and yoghurt, season with salt and chilli flakes, mix to combine, add the prawns and stir to evenly coat the prawns with the mixture, cover and leave to marinate for 1 hour. Place the breadcrumbs onto a plate, dip the marinated prawns in the breadcrumbs to coat, patting to ensure the prawns are evenly coated with the breadcrumbs. Heat some oil in a pan for deep frying and fry the prawns until golden brown.

Serve with a chutney of your choice.

Salt and Chilli Almonds
Serves 4

250g almonds in their skins
¼ cup oil
2 tsp chilli flakes
4 tbsp coarse salt

In a bowl, mix the almonds with the oil. Pour the almonds and oil into a roasting pan and spread the almonds to ensure they are evenly spaced. Roast for 30 minutes at 180°C until they have browned in colour. Keep checking and mixing to ensure they do not burn. When cooked, take out and place onto kitchen paper to drain. Transfer into a bowl and toss with coarse salt and chilli flakes.

Serve with drinks.
Optional: 1 tsp of toasted cumin powder can be added with, or instead of, chilli flakes

Potato Wedges
Serves 4

6 large potatoes
1 tsp cumin seeds, roasted and powdered in a blender
2 tsp chaat masala

Boil potatoes and cut into large wedges, leaving the skin on if wished. Place onto a baking tray. In bowl, mix together 4 tbsp oil with the cumin powder and season with salt and chilli flakes to taste, then pour over the potatoes. Bake in the oven for 30 minutes at 180°C, stirring once halfway through, and cook until they are crisp and golden. Remove into another bowl and sprinkle chaat masala over the top and toss to combine.

Serve.

Papdi

Serves 6

1 cup chapati flour
1 tsp carom seeds / ajwan or cumin seeds if preferred

Heat oil in a frying pan for deep frying. In a bowl add the flour and carom seeds, season with salt. Mix in water gradually, 1 tablespoon at a time, to form a dough. Knead the dough, which should not be too hard, but soft and manageable. Make 4 balls out of the dough and roll flat, using a small round cookie cutter, cut small rounds from the dough. Prick the small rounds with a fork to stop them puffing up. Drop them into the oil and deep fry until they are golden brown, turning them over in the oil. Remove onto kitchen paper to drain.

Serve.
Optional: Serve sprinkled with a little chaat masala and salt.

Sweet Chilli Biscuits

Serves 4

1 cup rice flour
1 cup plain flour
½ cup chapati flour
4 tbsp sugar

Mix the flours with sugar and season with 1 tsp salt and 1 tsp chilli flakes. Add 1 tbsp oil to the mixture and stir in. Slowly add some warm water to the mixture to form dough mixture. The dough should be soft but not sticky. Divide the dough into 3 or 4 balls, then roll these onto a floured work surface and cut sticks out of the dough. Heat oil in a frying pan and deep fry the cut pieces in oil until golden brown. Remove onto kitchen paper to drain. Sprinkle some sugar lightly onto the biscuits.

Serve.

Lamb and Pea Patties
Serves 4

250g minced lamb or beef
1 onion, chopped finely
1 cup frozen peas (or fresh)
2 tbsp curry paste

In a bowl, mix all the ingredients together and season with salt and chilli flakes. Cover and place in the fridge for about 1 hour. Shape the meat into small round patties. Heat 4 tbsp oil in a frying pan and add the patties to it. Fry, turning them over until the meat is cooked, about 5 minutes on each side. Remove from pan onto kitchen paper to drain.

Serve in pitta bread, drizzled with raita and / or mango chutney.

Chapati Toast
Serves 2

4 chapatis
4 tbsp mango chutney
4 tbsp cheddar cheese, grated
4 tbsp chopped coriander

Place the chapatis onto a baking tray and spoon 1 tbsp of mango chutney evenly on each chapatti. Sprinkle evenly with cheese, season with salt and chilli flakes. Sprinkle chopped coriander over the top. Cook in the oven at 180°C, until the cheese has melted and turned golden brown, about 10 – 15 minutes.

Serve.

Potato Crisps

Serves 4

4 potatoes, thinly sliced
2 tsp sea salt
2 tsp chilli flakes
2 tsp chaat masala

Heat oil for deep frying in a pan, add the thinly cut potato slices and fry until golden brown in colour and crisp. Drain onto kitchen paper. Place into a large bowl and sprinkle salt, chilli flakes and chaat masala over the crisps and toss to combine.

Serve.

Zucchini Flowers Filled With Paneer

Serves 4

8 zucchini flowers with the middle stamens removed
2 cups cooked scrambled paneer (see page 82)
2 tbsp lime juice

In a bowl, mix the cooked scrambled paneer with lime juice. Fill each zucchini flower with the paneer mixture and twist the top of the flower to secure, brush with a little oil. Place onto a greased baking tray and bake in the oven at 180°C for 30 minutes, turning to ensure all sides are cooked. Bake until slightly brown and cooked through.

Serve.

Grilled Romano Peppers
Serves 4

4 romano peppers
1 tbsp coriander chutney
1 tbsp oil

Slice the peppers lengthways and remove the inner seeds. Place the peppers on a baking tray and drizzle with oil. Place under a grill and turning often, grill until they are charred all over. Cool the peppers and remove the skin. Place onto a plate and drop a spoon of coriander chutney on top of each one.

Serve.

Paneer Pinwheels
Serves 4

4 slices white bread, with crusts removed
1 cup scrambled paneer (see page 82)
1 tbsp coriander, chopped
2 tbsp mango chutney

On a plate, lay out the slices of bread and spread with mango chutney. Add the scrambled paneer and sprinkle with coriander leaves. Roll the bread slices and secure with a toothpick. Cut them into slices and lay cut side up onto a plate.

Serve.

Paneer and Tomato Tarts

Serves 4

2 sheets ready-made puff pastry
1 cup scrambled paneer see page 82
2 tbsp dry roasted tomatoes
1 tbsp chopped fresh coriander

Cut the pastry sheets into 8 pieces. Place on to a baking tray and fold edges to make a crust. Prick the pastry with a fork. Bake in the oven at 180°C for 10 minutes. Remove from oven. In a bowl, mix the scrambled paneer with the tomatoes, season with salt and chilli flakes. Spread spoonfuls of this mixture onto the baked pastry cases. Sprinkle chopped coriander on top. Place back in the oven and bake for 10 minutes.

Serve.

Chicken and Chutney Sandwich

Serves 2

4 slices of bread with crusts removed if preferred
1 cup cooked chicken tikka (see page 40)
1 tbsp mango chutney

Place 2 slices of bread on a plate and spread mango chutney on the bread slices. Add the chicken pieces onto the bread. Sandwich the two slices together and cut in half.

Serve.

Tandoori Chicken Chapati Wrap
Serves 2

1 cup cooked chicken tikka (see page 40)
4 chapatis
4 tsp mint raita

Heat the chapatis and chicken tikka in a microwave until warm, about a minute for the chicken and 30 seconds for the chapati. Place the tandoori chicken pieces in the middle of the chapati, drizzle with raita and roll the chapati.

Serve.

Mint and Tomato Sandwich
Serves 2

4 white bread slices with crusts removed if preferred
4 tsp mint chutney (see page 163)
2 tomatoes sliced

Spread the mint chutney onto the bread slices and top with the sliced tomatoes. Place the second slice of bread on top to make a sandwich and cut in half.

Serve.

Spicy Potato Chapati Wraps
Serves 2

2 portions cooked cumin potatoes (see page 81)
4 tbsp mango chutney
4 chapatis

Heat the cumin potatoes in the microwave for about 1 minute and the chapati for about 30 seconds. Spread mango chutney on the chapatti, add the potatoes in the middle of the chapati and make into a roll.

Serve.

Paneer Toasty
Serves 2

1 cup cooked scrambled paneer (see page 82)
2 tbsp mango chutney
4 slices of white bread

Spread the mango chutney onto the bread slices and place the paneer in the middle of 2 slices of bread. Cover like a sandwich with the other slice. Lightly grease a toasted sandwich maker and place the stuffed bread slices onto the pan and close the lid. Cook for about 2 minutes until the bread has browned.

Serve.

Burger in a Roll
Serves 2

2 spicy cooked Indian beef burgers (see page 68)
2 tsp raita
2 burger buns
Mixed salad

Place the warm, spicy beef burger onto the bottom half of a bread bun. Top with salad, and drizzle with a little raita. Then add the top half of the bread bun.

Serve.
Optional: Replace the raita with spicy mango chutney.

Spicy Corn on the Cob
Serves 2

2 corn cobs
4 tbsp melted butter
1 tsp cumin powder
1 tsp coriander paste

In a small bowl, mix together the melted butter, with cumin powder and coriander paste, season with salt and chilli flakes, keep aside. Cook the corn as desired, either under a grill or on a barbecue. In both cases, turn often. When cooked and slightly browned, spread with the melted butter mixture.

Serve.

Paneer Bruschetta
Serves 2

1 cup diced fresh tomatoes
½ cup red onion, diced finely
½ cup paneer diced (see page 80)
2 tbsp tamarind chutney

In a small frying pan heat 2 tbsp of oil, add the paneer cubes and sauté for about 2 minutes, until golden brown in colour. Remove and place in a bowl with the diced red onion and tomatoes, season with salt and chilli flakes, stir to mix together. To make the bruschetta, cut 4 slices from a baguette and place under the grill for a few minutes until browned, turn the bread over and drizzle with a little olive oil over the top and grill again to brown. Remove from the grill and place the bruschetta onto a plate with the oiled side on top. Spread evenly with the paneer and tomato mixtures, finally drizzle with tamarind chutney.

Serve.

Tandoori Pizza
Serves 4

2 large pizza bases
1 jar tomato pizza sauce
2 cups cooked tandoori chicken tikka pieces (see page 40)
1 cup cheddar cheese, grated

Place the pizza base onto a baking tray and spread the tomato pizza sauce over the base. Add the chicken pieces, spreading evenly over the pizza. Sprinkle cheese over the top and season with salt and chilli flakes. Bake in the oven for 30 minutes at 180°C until the cheese has melted.

Serve with coriander leaves as garnish.

Fried Sardines

Serves 4

8 sardines
1 tsp turmeric powder
2 tbsp lime juice

In a bowl, mix the turmeric and lime juice and season with salt and chilli flakes to make a paste. Add the sardines to the paste and mix to coat, marinate the sardines in the paste for 1 hour. Heat 1 tbsp of oil in a frying pan; add the sardines to the pan with the marinade. Cook on one side and then turn them over and cook the other side.

Serve.

Almond Crabs

Serves 4

500g crabmeat, all cartilage and shell removed. Alternatively, use tinned crabmeat
100g flaked almonds
125ml double cream
1 tbsp chopped coriander leaves

In a frying pan, heat 1 tbsp of oil. Add the almonds and cook until they change to a golden brown colour. Remove and keep aside. Heat 2 tbsp of oil in the pan and add the crabmeat. Cook for about 10 minutes, stirring often, until the crabmeat has browned. Stir the almonds into the crabmeat and add ¼ cup water, season with salt and chilli flakes. Mix in the cream, and bring to the boil, lower heat and simmer stirring until all the liquid has evaporated. Add the coriander leaves and stir, remove from heat.

Serve.

Lime and Chilli Salmon Wraps
Serves 2

2 salmon steaks
2 tbsp lime juice
2 tbsp tandoori tikka paste
4 chapatis

In a frying pan, heat 1 tbsp of oil. When hot, add the tandoori paste, lime juice and ¼ cup water, season with salt and chilli flakes. Bring to the boil. Cut the salmon into bite size pieces and gently place in the pan. Lower the heat and cook the salmon, stirring often but making sure not to break the salmon pieces. Heat the chapati in a grill or in a microwave for 30 seconds to warm, and then place onto a plate. Place the salmon into the middle and roll to form a wrap.

Serve.
Optional: Serve salmon drizzled with raita, with salad leaves enclosed in the wrap.

Tuna and Chilli Angel Pasta
Serves 4

1 large can of tuna in oil
250g angel hair pasta
400g tinned chopped tomatoes
2 tsp cumin seeds

Cook angel hair pasta as per packet instructions and keep aside. In a frying pan, heat 2 tbsp oil, add the cumin seeds and cook until they turn a dark brown colour. Add the tomatoes, and cook stirring for about 1 minute, season with salt and chilli flakes. Add the tuna and ¼ cup water, bring to boil, then lower the heat and simmer until the water has evaporated and the tuna is cooked. Pour the cooked pasta into the pan with the tuna and stir. Remove into a large bowl.

Serve sprinkled with coriander.

Kumara (Sweet Potato) and Pumpkin Soup

Serves 4

500g pumpkin, finely chopped
1 small kumara, chopped
400ml tin coconut cream
1 tbsp curry paste

Place all the ingredients into a saucepan with 3 cups of water. Season with salt, bring to boil and lower the heat and simmer until the vegetables become soft. The soup should thicken a little. When cooked cool the soup a little, then pour all the ingredients into a blender and blend until smooth.

Serve.

Lentil and Carrot Soup

Serves 4

2 x 400g tinned brown lentils
2 tbsp curry paste
4 carrots, diced
2 tbsp lime juice

In a frying pan, heat 1 tbsp oil and add the curry paste. Cook for about 1 minute, then add the diced carrots and cook for about 1 minute, stirring often. Add the lentils and 1 cup water, season with salt and chilli flakes. Bring to boil and then lower the heat and simmer until the vegetables are cooked and soup has thickened. When the soup is cooked, stir in the lime juice.

Serve.

Egg Curry
Serves 2

4 hardboiled eggs, cut into halves
1 onion, finely chopped
2 tbsp curry paste
200g tinned chopped tomatoes

In a saucepan heat 2 tbsp of oil, add the chopped onions cook until they have browned. Add the curry paste and chopped tomatoes, season with salt and chilli flakes. Cook for 5 minutes to release the flavors, then add ½ cup of water and bring to boil, lower heat and simmer gently for 30 minutes or until the water has evaporated and the curry takes on a sauce consistency. Drop the boiled eggs in and stir, ensuring that the eggs do not break. Cook for a further 2 minutes without stirring.

Serve with chapati.

Spicy Jacket Potato
Serves 2

2 baking potatoes
4 tbsp spicy coleslaw (see page 157)

Wash the potatoes to remove any soil, and pat dry with a tea towel and rub a little oil onto each potato. Place 1 tsp of salt on a plate and roll the potatoes in the salt to give them a little covering of salt, this will ensure they are crispy on the outside. Next prick them all over with a fork. Place onto a baking tray and bake in the oven at 180°C for 1 hour until cooked, they should be soft in the middle when touched. Take out of the oven and slit open with a knife. Spoon the spicy coleslaw on the top.

Serve.

Aloo Tikki (Potato Patty)
Serves 2

2 potatoes boiled and mashed
1 cup fresh or frozen peas
1 tsp cumin powder
1 tsp mango powder

In a bowl add all the ingredients, season with salt and chilli flakes to taste, and mix to combine. Shape the mixture into small round patties about 3-4 depending on the size of the patties. Place oil into a frying pan so that the bottom of the pan is covered in oil and heat. The patties should be shallow fried. Add the patties into the pan and cook until one side is browned, gently turn over and cook and brown the other side. Remove onto to kitchen paper to drain.

Serve with chutney of your choice.

Meals

Chicken

Lamb

Pork

Beef

Seafood

Vegetarian

Marinades and Pastes

Eating good food with family and friends is an enjoyable experience, as well as providing the nutrients we need. The recipes for meals used are simple, easy and full of flavour. This will allow you to spend time doing what you enjoy in this book but still create meals that will wow your family and friends. The recipes here are authentic Indian cuisine which is enjoyed in my household and many others.

Dinner

The evening dinner is when the whole family eats together. At the start of the meal, all the different dishes are placed in the centre of the table and family members can choose which to spoon onto their plate, or into the small bowls on their own thali plates. The word 'thali' refers to the large plate that contains the individual's own selections. A thali will have everything you need for a well-balanced meal and will often contain the starters as well as the main meal.

A thali dinner consists of dishes which complement each other and a typical meal would often include the following:

- Rice
- Chapati
- Meat dish
- Vegetable dish
- Dhal dish
- Raita
- Salad
- Chutney

A vegetarian will take out the meat dish and add another one or two vegetable dishes. A thali is always accompanied by plenty of papadums, which are wafer-thin crispy snacks. However, they can also be served as a starter with dips or toppings. In some regions of India they are served at the end of a meal. Papadums can be enjoyed as a snack between meals too.

Chicken

Spicy Arabiatta Chicken
Serves 2

2 chicken breasts, diced
1 large jar of arabiatta sauce
1 tbsp cumin seeds
2 tsp garam masala

In a frying pan, heat a little oil and brown the diced chicken for a few minutes, then keep aside. In another saucepan, heat about 2 tbsp of olive oil and fry the cumin seeds for about 1 minute until they become fragrant and change colour. Pour in the arabiatta sauce season with salt and chilli flakes, add 2 tbsp water, and cook for about 2 minutes stirring. Add the browned chicken with ½ cup water and the garam masala, stir and bring to boil. Lower heat and simmer for about 10 minutes, giving an occasional stir, until the chicken is cooked.

Serve with cooked pasta spirals and a salad.

Sweet Chilli Chicken
Serves 2

2 chicken breasts
2 tbsp honey
4 tbsp sweet chilli sauce
2 tbsp lemon juice

In a bowl, mix together the honey, sweet chilli sauce and lemon juice. Wrap each chicken breast in cling film and flatten using a wooden meat mallet. Once the chicken is flattened, make small slashes in the chicken breast and brush the sauce thickly on both sides. Heat 2 tbsp of oil in a frying pan and cook the chicken on both sides until cooked through.

Serve.

Easy Tandoori Chicken
Serves 2

2 chicken breasts, with skin removed
4 tbsp tandoori curry paste
2 tbsp plain yoghurt

In a bowl, mix the tandoori paste with the plain yoghurt, season with salt and chilli flakes. Make slashes in the chicken with a knife, and cover with the paste mixture. Cover and leave in the fridge to marinate for 2 hours or overnight if possible. Place the chicken onto a greased baking tray and bake in the oven at 180°C for 30 to 40 minutes until the chicken is cooked through. Turn over halfway through cooking. Alternatively, the chicken can be barbecued.

Serve with a green salad and raita of your choice.

Spicy Mango Chicken
Serves 2

2 chicken breasts, with skin removed
4 tbsp mango chutney
1 tbsp cumin seeds
2 tbsp tandoori curry paste

In a bowl, mix the mango chutney with cumin seeds, season with salt and chilli flakes. Make a deep pocket on the top of each chicken breast and place the mango chutney mixture into the slash. Seal with toothpicks to secure. Brush the curry paste onto the chicken breast and leave covered in the fridge to marinate for about 3 hours or longer if you have time. Heat the oven to 180°C degrees and place the chicken breasts onto a greased baking tray and bake for 30-40 minutes until cooked through. Remove toothpicks before serving.

Serve with a salad.

Easy Chicken Curry
Serves 2

2 chicken breasts, cut into bite-size pieces
½ jar curry paste
1 onion, finely chopped
½ tin chopped tomatoes

In a frying pan, heat 2 tbsp oil and add the chopped onions and cook until they brown. Add the curry paste and chopped tomatoes, season with salt and chilli flakes. Add ¼ cup water and cook the mixture until the water has evaporated, stirring often. Add the chicken pieces and 1 cup water and bring to boil, whilst stirring. Lower heat and simmer gently, giving an occasional stir until the chicken is cooked and the sauce has reduced.

Serve with naan bread and rice, with chopped coriander as garnish.

Lime and Chilli Chicken
Serves 2

1 chicken breast, with skin removed and cut into strips
Juice of 1 lime
2 tbsp sweet chilli sauce

In a bowl, mix the sweet chilli sauce and the juice of 1 lime, season with salt and chilli flakes to taste. Add the strips of chicken to the sauce and mix to coat. Cover and leave in fridge for at least an hour. Place the chicken strips onto a greased tray individually and bake in the oven at 180°C for 30 minutes, or until the chicken is cooked.

Serve with a green salad or in wraps.

Lime and Chilli Chicken Wrap
Serves 2

Cooked lime and chilli chicken pieces (see page 38)
4 chapatis
A few green salad leaves
4 tbsp raita

Place the chapatis onto a plate, add the lime and chilli chicken in the middle with a few green salad leaves and drizzle with raita. Roll the chapatis tightly.

Serve.

Chicken with Sun Dried Tomatoes
Serves 2

2 chicken breasts, with skin removed
2 tbsp sundried tomatoes
2 tsp dry roasted cumin seeds
2 tbsp lime juice

Place the sundried tomatoes in a bowl, with a little of their own oil, mix with the toasted cumin seeds and lime juice and season with salt and chilli flakes, and keep aside. Lay the chicken breasts out and flatten with a meat mallet. They need to be fairly thin, about 1 inch thick. Spread the prepared tomato mixture onto the chicken breasts and roll to seal and secure with toothpicks. Place onto a greased baking tray, drizzle a little olive oil over the chicken and sprinkle with some salt and chilli flakes. Bake in the oven at 180°C, for 30 minutes, until the chicken is cooked through. Remove onto a plate and cut in slices, removing the toothpicks.

Serve with a green salad.

Chicken Tikka

Serves 2

1 chicken breast, diced into bite-size pieces
2 tbsp tandoori tikka paste

In a frying pan, heat 1 tbsp of oil, add the tandoori tikka paste along with 2 tbsp water. Stir and cook for about 1 minute. Add the chicken pieces and mix, adding ¼ cup of water. Stir continually to prevent the chicken from sticking to the pan. Add more water should the mixture become dry. Cook on a low heat until the chicken is cooked through and the water has evaporated. Remove onto a plate.

Serve with a green salad drizzled with raita.

Chicken Pakoras

Serves 2

Portion of chicken tikka pieces (see recipe above)
1 cup besan (chickpea flour)
Plain flour

In a bowl, add the besan and season with salt and chilli flakes. Add water gradually, 1 tbsp at a time, to make a thick batter (add water slowly as the besan tends to become thin quite quickly). Place a little flour onto a plate and dust the chicken pieces with the flour. Place enough oil into a frying pan to deep fry. Dip the chicken pieces into the besan batter and deep fry in the oil. When they are golden brown in colour, drain onto kitchen paper.

Serve.

Chicken and Mixed Pepper Curry
Serves 2

2 chicken breasts, cut into bite size pieces.
1 jar of Indian curry sauce of your choice
Green, red and yellow peppers, cut into strips
½ cup dried fenugreek leaves

Chargrill the peppers by drizzling some oil over them and place under a grill, turning frequently. Cook until the skin on both sides is slightly charred. In a frying pan heat a little oil then brown the chicken pieces. Add the curry sauce, the fenugreek leaves, the chargrilled peppers and ½ cup water, season with salt and chilli flakes. Stir and bring to the boil, then lower the heat and simmer gently until the chicken is cooked and a thick sauce remains.

Serve with rice.

Chicken Kebabs
Serves 2

2 chicken breasts, diced
2 tbsp tandoori tikka masala paste
4 tbsp plain yoghurt
2 tbsp fresh chopped coriander

In a bowl, add the plain yoghurt and beat well. Add the tandoori tikka masala paste and the coriander, season with salt and chilli flakes to taste. Add the chicken pieces and mix well. Cover and leave in the fridge to marinate for 2 hours or longer if possible. Thread the chicken pieces onto pre-soaked bamboo skewers and grill under a hot grill or barbecue until the chicken is cooked through.

Serve with a green salad.

Tandoori Chicken and Mint

Serves 2

2 chicken breasts
2 tbsp tandoori paste
4 tbsp plain yoghurt
1 tbsp thick mint sauce

In a bowl, mix the tandoori paste with the plain yoghurt and mint sauce, season with salt and chilli flakes. Make slashes in the chicken breast and place in the marinade, ensuring the marinade covers all the chicken. Cover and leave in the fridge for 2 hours or overnight if possible. Place the chicken onto a greased baking tray and bake in the oven at 180°C for 30 minutes or until the chicken is cooked, turning over once midway through.

Serve.

Optional: Chicken can be sliced and used in a salad

Chicken Breasts with Mint Sauce
Serves 2

2 chicken breasts
2 cups yoghurt
½ cucumber
2 tbsp mint sauce

Make deep slashes in the chicken breasts with a knife. Place in a bowl with 1 cup yoghurt, season with salt and chilli flakes to taste. Mix to ensure the chicken is covered with the yoghurt. Cover and place in the fridge to marinate for an hour or longer if possible. In a bowl, mix 1 cup of yoghurt with the cucumber and mint sauce, season with salt and chilli flakes. When marinated, place the chicken breasts onto a greased oven tray and bake for 30 minutes at 180°C turning over once during cooking. When cooked, remove onto a plate and spoon the mint and cucumber yoghurt dressing over the top.

Serve.

Fried Chicken
Serves 2

2 chicken breasts, diced
4 tbsp tandoori tikka paste
½ cup plain yoghurt
1 tbsp lemon juice

In a bowl, mix the tandoori paste with the lemon juice and yoghurt. Add the chicken pieces, cover and marinate for 2 hours or longer if possible. Deep fry the chicken pieces in oil until they are cooked and have turned a deep red colour.

Serve drizzled with lemon juice and lemon wedges.

Coriander Chicken
Serves 4

2 chicken breasts, diced
½ cup fresh cream
1 tbsp coriander paste
1 tbsp mint leaves

Note: If coriander or mint leaves are unavailable, use paste.

In a bowl, mix together the cream, coriander and mint with 1 tbsp of oil, season with salt and chilli flakes to taste. Add the chicken and mix to coat them in the mixture. Leave to marinate for 2 hours or longer if possible. Heat oil in a frying pan and add the chicken with the marinade and ¼ cup water. Cook until the chicken is cooked through, stirring often until the water has evaporated.

Serve with lemon wedges.

Garlic and Chilli Chicken
Serves 4

2 chicken breasts
½ tsp garlic paste
1 cup yoghurt
1 tsp paprika powder

In a bowl, mix together the yoghurt, garlic and paprika with 1 tbsp of oil, season with salt and chilli flakes to taste. Make slashes in the chicken breast and coat with the marinade. Leave to marinate in the fridge for 2 hours or longer if possible. Grill or barbeque chicken breasts until cooked through, turning a few times and basting with any leftover marinade.

Serve with lemon wedges.

Whole Roast Chicken with Cumin and Lemon
Serves 4

1 whole roasting chicken
2 lemons
1 tbsp cumin powder

In a bowl, mix 2 tbsp oil with the cumin, lemon rind from one lemon and 2 tbsp lemon juice, season with salt and chilli flakes. Rub mixture all over the chicken. Cut the other lemon into wedges and place into the chicken cavity. Place the chicken in a roasting dish with a little oil. Roast the chicken for 1 hour and 30 minutes at 180°C, or until cooked.

Serve.

Lemon Chicken
Serves 2

2 chicken breasts
¼ cup lemon juice
Pinch of turmeric powder
1 tsp of cumin powder

In a bowl, mix together the lemon juice, turmeric, cumin powder, season with salt and chilli flakes to taste. Make slashes in the chicken breasts and add to the marinade, ensuring they are well covered. Leave in fridge for a minimum of 1 hour. Cook the chicken on the grill, turning over halfway through until the chicken is cooked. Alternatively place onto a greased baking tray and bake in the oven at 180°C for about 35 to 40 minutes until cooked through, turning over during cooking.

Serve.

Buttermilk Marinated Chicken
Serves 2

2 chicken breasts, cut into strips
1 cup buttermilk
1 tbsp curry paste
1 cup flour

In a bowl, add buttermilk and curry paste, season with salt and chilli flakes to taste and mix together. Heat some oil in a frying pan. Dust the chicken with the flour and then dip into the buttermilk and curry mixture and fry the chicken until cooked through and golden brown in colour. Remove and place onto kitchen paper to drain.

Serve with lemon wedges.

Chilli and Honey Chicken Drumsticks
Serves 2

4 chicken drumsticks
4 tbsp honey
4 tbsp lime juice
2 tsp chilli powder / paste

In a bowl, mix the honey, chilli and lime juice, season with a little salt. Place chicken into the mixture and coat. Grill the chicken, turning a few times to cook evenly. Alternatively, the chicken can be barbecued.

Serve with salad.

Chicken Marinated in Yoghurt
Serves 2

4 chicken drumsticks
1 cup yoghurt
1 tbsp lemon juice
1 tbsp coriander paste

In a bowl, mix yoghurt with lemon juice, coriander and season with a little salt and chilli flakes to taste. Add the chicken and mix to coat. Cover and marinate in the fridge for 2 hours or longer if possible. Grill the chicken, turning a few times to cook evenly. Alternatively, the chicken can be barbecued.

Serve with salad.

Roast Chicken
Serves 2

1 roasting chicken
1 tsp cumin powder
1 tsp coriander powder

In a bowl mix the cumin and coriander powders together. Brush the chicken with oil and sprinkle the spices over the chicken, patting to ensure they stick to the chicken. Pour a little oil in a roasting tin and place the chicken into the tin. Roast the chicken in a pre-heated oven at 180°C for approximately 1 hour, or until the chicken is cooked.

Serve with roast potatoes and vegetables.

Chicken and Pineapple
Serves 2

2 chicken breasts, cut in cubes
400g tinned pineapple pieces (in their own juice)
2 tbsp sugar
2 tsp curry powder

In a bowl, mix the pineapple juice from the tinned pineapple, sugar, curry powder, season with salt and chilli flakes. Add the chicken breast pieces and mix to coat. Cover and leave to marinate in fridge for 1 hour or longer if possible. Soak bamboo skewers in water, and alternately thread the chicken and pineapple pieces onto the skewers. Grill until the chicken is cooked and a little charred. Alternatively, the skewers can be barbecued.

Serve.

Chicken and Coconut
Serves 4

4 chicken breasts, cut into bite-size pieces
400ml can coconut cream
1 tbsp cumin seeds
1 ½ tbsp curry powder

In a bowl, mix the coconut cream with 1 cup water and curry powder, season with salt and chilli flakes. Keep aside. Heat a little oil in a frying pan. Brown the chicken pieces, then remove and keep aside. In the frying pan, add the cumin seeds and fry until they change colour. Add the coconut mixture and bring to boil. Add the chicken, stirring often. Reduce heat to a simmer and cook until the sauce thickens and the chicken is cooked.

Serve sprinkled with chopped coriander.
Optional: Add 2 tbsp lemon juice and stir before removing from heat.

Chicken with Pomegranate
Serves 2

2 chicken breasts, diced
2 tbsp dried pomegranate powder
1 tsp curry powder
1 tsp ginger and garlic paste (see page 91)

In a bowl, combine the chicken with all the remaining ingredients. Marinate for 2 hours or overnight if possible. In a saucepan, add 4 tbsp of oil, then pour in all the marinade along with the chicken, season with salt and chilli flakes to taste and add 1 cup of water. Bring to boil lower heat and simmer until the chicken is cooked and the water has completely evaporated, stirring continually.

Serve with chopped coriander.

Garlic Chicken
Serves 2

2 chicken breasts
2 tsp curry powder
2 tbsp soy sauce
½ tsp garlic paste

In a bowl, mix 4 tbsp oil with soy sauce, garlic paste and turmeric. Make slashes in the chicken breasts and add to the turmeric mixture. Coat the chicken well. Place chicken onto a baking tray and bake in the oven at 180°C for 45 minutes or until the chicken is browned and thoroughly cooked.

Serve.
Optional: Chicken can be sliced and used in a salad

Lamb

Mince Curry (keema)
Serves 2

500g mince lamb / beef
2 heaped tbsp curry paste
1 onion, chopped
200g tinned chopped tomatoes with garlic

In a saucepan heat 2 tbsp of oil, add the chopped onions and cook until browned. Add the curry paste and cook for 1 minute. Add the tomatoes and season with salt and chilli flakes, add ¼ cup of water, and bring to boil stirring. Cook until the water has evaporated and a thick sauce remains. Add the mince with ½ cup water and bring to boil stirring, breaking the lumps formed in the mince. Lower the heat and simmer, stirring often until all the liquid has evaporated and the mince is cooked.

Serve: garnished with coriander leaves and rice.
Optional: Throw in a handful of frozen peas with the mince when cooking.
Optional: Use as a filling in samasas.

Indian Cottage Pie
Serves 2

Cooked mince curry (see page 51)
4 potatoes, boiled and mashed
2 tsp cumin powder
1 tbsp fresh coriander leaves, chopped

In an ovenproof dish, add the lamb curry. In a bowl, mix the mashed potatoes, cumin and chopped coriander, season with salt and chilli flakes. Spread the mashed potatoes over the mince and place in the oven at 180°C for 30 minutes.

Serve.
Optional: Mix a dash of milk and butter for a creamy mashed potato topping.

Mince with Cheesy Potatoes
Serves 2

Cooked mince curry (see page 51)
2 potatoes, thinly sliced
½ cup cheese
2 tbsp milk

In an ovenproof dish, add the mince curry. Layer the sliced potatoes over the mince and pour the milk over the potatoes. In a bowl mix the grated cheese with salt and chilli flakes to taste. Sprinkle the seasoned cheese on top of the potatoes. Place in a pre-heated oven at 180°C for 30 minutes until cooked and the cheese has melted.

Serve with salad.

Marinated Lamb Chops
Serves 2

4 lamb chops
2 tbsp curry powder
1 tsp honey

In a bowl, mix together the curry powder and honey with 1 tbsp oil, season with salt and chilli flakes. Rub mixture over the lamb chops and marinate in fridge for 2 hours or longer if possible. Grill or barbecue, according to your liking.

Serve.

Minty Lamb Chops
Serves 2

4 lamb chops
1 cup mint raita (see page 147)
1 tsp garam masala
1 tbsp fresh chopped coriander

In a bowl, mix the mint raita, garam masala and chopped coriander with 1 tbsp of oil, season with salt and chilli flakes. Pour over the lamb chops and mix to coat. Leave in fridge to marinate for 2 hours or longer if possible. Grill or barbecue, according to your liking.

Serve.

Minty Lamb Curry
Serves 2

200g lamb, cut into cubes
2 heaped tbsp madras curry paste
200g tinned chopped tomatoes with garlic
1 bunch of fresh mint leaves, chopped

In a saucepan, heat 2 tbsp of oil, add the curry paste and tomatoes with ¼ cup water, season with salt. Cook stirring to release the flavours, until the water has evaporated. Add the lamb cubes with 1 cup water and stir. Bring to the boil, then lower the heat and simmer until meat is tender and cooked. Keep stirring often and if the mixture becomes dry, add some more water. The gravy should be thick and paste-like. When the lamb is cooked, add the mint leaves and cook for a further 3 minutes, stirring often.

Serve with rice.

Lamb Curry with Fenugreek
Serves 2

200g lamb, cubed
1 jar of any curry cooking sauce
½ cup dried fenugreek leaves / kasoori methi
1 tsp garam masala

In a saucepan, brown the lamb in 2 tbsp of oil, and then add the curry sauce and 1 cup of water. Bring to the boil and simmer gently until the lamb is cooked and the water has evaporated, leaving a thick sauce. Add the fenugreek leaves and garam masala, and cook for a further 2 minutes, stirring continually.

Serve with rice.

Pomegranate Lamb Chops
Serves 2

4 lamb chops
2 tbsp pomegranate powder
4 tbsp olive oil
1 tsp garlic

In a bowl, mix the pomegranate powder, oil and garlic, season with salt and chilli flakes. Add the lamb chops and cover with the mixture. Leave to marinate in the fridge for at least 4 hours. On a baking sheet, spray some oil. Place the chops on the sheet and bake in the oven at 180°C for 30 to 40 minutes. Turn over halfway through the cooking process.

Serve.

Lamb Pie
Serves 2

200g lamb mince curry (see page 51)
1 sheet of butter puff pastry
1 egg, beaten

Preheat oven at 180°C. Divide the lamb mince curry into 2 individual pie dishes. Cut the pastry sheets to fit the pie dish and cover the dish as a lid. Squeeze the edges to form a seal. Use some of the bits of pastry to make a pattern on top of the pie. Brush the pastry with the beaten egg. Bake in the oven for 40 minutes, at 180°C.

Serve.

Fenugreek Lamb Chops
Serves 2

6 lamb chops
2 tbsp dried fenugreek leaves / kasoori methi
50ml plain yoghurt
2 tsp garam masala

In a bowl, add the yoghurt and mix with the garam masala, fenugreek leaves and 1 tbsp. of oil, season with salt and chilli flakes. Pour over the lamb chops and mix to coat the chops, place in the fridge to marinate for 2 hours or overnight if possible. Pre-heat the oven to 180°C. Place chops on a greased baking tray and cook, to your liking. Alternatively, barbecue the chops on the grill.

Serve with a salad.

Lamb Chops Curry
Serves 2

4 lamb chops
½ jar tandoori curry sauce
2 tbsp single cream
1 tsp garam masala

Brush some oil on both sides of the lamb chops, season with salt and chilli flakes to taste. Place in a frying pan and cook to your liking or alternatively they can be grilled. Remove the chops onto a plate. In a saucepan add the curry sauce and ¼cup water, bring to boil. Add the lamb chops, cream and garam masala to the pan. Lower the heat and simmer gently until the water has evaporated.

Serve with rice.

Kebabs
Serves 4

250g lean minced lamb or beef
2 tbsp tandoori curry paste
1 egg
1 cup breadcrumbs

In a bowl, mix all the ingredients together and leave in the fridge for 1 hour. Make long sausage shapes and thread onto bamboo skewers (soak the bamboo skewers in water first). Grill on a barbecue or in the oven until the meat is cooked. Place onto a plate and remove the skewers.

Serve in warm pitta bread, with raita drizzled on top.

Buttered Lamb Roast
Serves 2

4 sliced pieces of cooked roast lamb
½ tbsp cumin seeds
½ tbsp mustard seeds
1 tbsp dried fenugreek leaves

In a frying pan, heat 1 tbsp oil. Add the cumin and mustard seeds, fry for about 1 minute or until they pop. Add the dried fenugreek leaves and cook for 1 minute. Spoon the mixture over the slices of roast lamb.

Serve.

Honey and Tamarind Lamb Kebabs
Serves 2

500g lamb, cut into cubes
½ cup honey
3 tbsp chilli and garlic sauce (see page 92)
3 tbsp tamarind paste

In a bowl, mix the honey, chilli and garlic sauce and tamarind paste, adding salt to taste. Mix in the cubed meat and leave to marinate for about 1 hour. Thread the meat onto pre-soaked bamboo skewers, then grill or barbecue to liking. Place onto a plate and remove the skewers.

Serve.

Honey Cumin and Mint Lamb Chops
Serves 2

6 lamb chops
2 tbsp mint sauce
1 tsp cumin seeds, roasted
2 tbsp honey

In a frying pan, dry roast the cumin seeds until they change colour. In a bowl, mix together the honey, mint sauce and roasted cumin seeds, season with salt and chilli flakes. Brush the mixture over the lamb chops and marinate in the fridge for 1 hour. Grill or bake in the oven on a greased baking tray for 20 minutes at 180°C.

Serve.

Lamb Biryani
Serves 4

500g lamb, diced
3 tbsp balti curry paste
1 cup basmati rice
Handful of unsalted cashew nuts

Wash rice in several changes of water and keep to one side. In a small frying pan, dry roast the cashew nuts and keep aside. In a saucepan, heat 2 tbsp of oil and fry the lamb cubes for about 15 minutes until they are browned. Add the balti curry paste and 1 cup of water, bring to the boil, lower heat and simmer, stirring often until the water has evaporated. Add the rice and stir in 1 ½ cups of water. Bring to the boil and lower heat, simmering gently for about 20 minutes or until the rice and meat is cooked. Add the cashew nuts and fluff the rice.

Serve with raita and a salad.

Sesame Seed Lamb Chops
Serves 4

8 lamb chops, trimmed of all fat
1 tbsp sesame seeds
½ cup yoghurt
1 tbsp curry powder

In a bowl, mix the yoghurt with curry powder and 1 tbsp of oil, season with salt and chilli flakes. Add the lamb chops to the yoghurt mixture, and marinate in the fridge for at least 2 hours, longer if possible. Sprinkle sesame seeds over the lamb chops and grill to your liking.

Serve.

Lamb Patties
Serves 4

250g lean mince lamb or beef
2 tbsp tandoori curry paste
½ onion, chopped finely
1 cup breadcrumbs

In a bowl, mix all the ingredients together and leave in the fridge for 1 hour. Make patties out of the mixture. Grill on a barbecue or in an oven until the meat is cooked.

Serve in warm bread buns or pitta bread, drizzled with mint raita on top.

Pork

Chilli Glazed Pork Chops
Serves 2

4 pork chops
1 tbsp sugar
1 tbsp chilli flakes
1 tsp cumin seeds

In a small bowl, mix the sugar, chilli flakes, and cumin seeds with 2 tbsp oil, season with salt. Brush the mixture onto the pork chops and grill for 7 minutes or to your liking. Turn the chops over, brush the other side with the mixture, and grill until cooked to liking.

Serve with a green salad, drizzled with raita of choice.

Chilli and Lemon Pork Chops
Serves 2

4 pork chops
1 lemon
1 tbsp oil
1 tsp cumin seeds

In a frying pan, dry roast the cumin seeds until they release their aroma. Crush seeds in a pestle and mortar. Grate the rind of the lemon, preserving the juice. In a small bowl, mix the lemon juice and rind with the crushed cumin seeds and 1 tbsp oil, season with salt and chilli flakes to taste. Brush the mixture onto the pork chops and grill for 8 minutes. Turn the chops over, brush the other side and grill until done.

Serve with a green salad, drizzled with raita of choice.

Pork and Mango Curry
Serves 2

1 jar spicy mango chutney
6 pork chops
½ onion, finely chopped
2 tsp curry powder

Sprinkle a little oil onto the pork chops and season with salt and chilli flakes, then leave to marinate for about an hour. In a frying pan, heat 2 tbsp oil and fry the onions until brown. Add the curry powder and cook for about 1 minute to release the flavours. Add the spicy mango chutney with ½ cup water, bring to boil, lower the heat and simmer, until the water has evaporated and the sauce is reduced by half. Grill the pork chops to your liking. When the sauce has reduced by half, add the pork chops to the sauce and stir to mix, bringing to the boil. Cook for another 1 - 2 minutes.

Serve with rice and vegetables.

Spicy Pork Chops
Serves 1

2 pork chops
1 lime
1 tbsp honey
½ tsp garlic paste

Grate the zest of the lime, preserving the juice. In a bowl, mix together the lime zest and juice with honey and garlic paste, season with salt and chilli flakes. Pour over the pork chops and marinate in the fridge for 1 hour or longer if possible. Place onto a baking tray and bake for 25 minutes in a 180°C oven, turning occasionally until cooked.

Serve.

Pork Skewers
Serves 4

500g boneless pork, cut into cubes
2 tbsp curry powder
1 tbsp chopped coriander leaves or paste

Place pork pieces into a dish and keep aside. In a bowl, mix 2 tbsp oil with the curry powder and coriander, season with salt and chilli flakes. Pour over the pork and mix to coat. Marinate overnight in the fridge. The next day, remove from fridge and stir the pork pieces. Thread onto pre-soaked bamboo skewers, and grill or barbecue, turning and basting as you cook the pork. Cook to your preference. Transfer onto a plate, removing the skewers.

Serve.

Cashew Nut Crumbed Pork
Serves 4

4 pork medallions
1 cup roasted cashews, finely chopped
½ cup breadcrumbs
1 tsp cumin seeds

In a bowl, mix chopped cashews, breadcrumbs and cumin seeds, season with salt and chilli flakes. Keep aside. In a frying pan, add 2 tbsp oil and cook the pork chops lightly to seal. Remove onto a plate. When cooled, dip chops in the cashew and breadcrumb mixture, ensuring both sides are covered with the crumbs. Heat 2 tbsp oil in a frying pan, and cook the pork until golden brown and thoroughly cooked.

Serve.

Chilli Pork and Pears
Serves 4

4 pork chops
2 pears sliced
1 red onion, cut into slices
½ cup sweet chilli sauce

In a frying pan, heat 2 tbsp of oil. Add the pork chops, sprinkle with salt and chilli flakes, and cook to your liking. Remove onto a plate. Add the onions to a frying pan with another 2 tbsp oil and cook until the onions turn a golden brown colour. Add pears to the pan with the sweet chilli sauce. Stir and season with salt and chilli flakes, add ¼ cup of water. Bring to the boil and simmer until the water has evaporated and the pears are soft. Pour the sauce over the pork chops.

Serve.

Tamarind and Date Pork
Serves 4

500g pork fillet, sliced
½ cup date and tamarind chutney see page 160
½ onion thinly sliced

In a frying pan, add 2 tbsp oil and brown the pork fillets in batches on a medium heat. Remove and keep aside. Add the onions to the pan and cook until golden brown. Return the pork to the pan with the date and tamarind chutney and ½ cup water, season with salt and chilli flakes. Bring to the boil and simmer gently until the pork is cooked, and the water has evaporated.

Serve.

Beef

Steak with Pomegranate
Serves 2

2 steaks
1 tsp garam masala
2 tsp pomegranate powder

In a bowl, mix the garam masala and pomegranate powder with a 1 tbsp olive oil, season with salt and chilli flakes to taste. Add the steaks and mix with the marinade, then leave to marinate for at least an hour. Heat a little oil in a pan and cook the steaks to your liking. Alternatively, they can be barbecued.

Serve.

Spicy Steak
Serves 2

2 tenderloin steaks
1 tbsp curry paste
1 tsp coriander seeds
1 tsp cumin seeds

Dry fry the coriander and cumin seeds in a frying pan until they release their flavour, then crush in a pestle and mortar. In a bowl mix 1 tbsp oil with the curry paste, season with salt and chilli flakes to taste. Brush the mixture over the steaks on both sides. Sprinkle the crushed seeds onto the steaks. Heat a little oil in a pan and cook the steaks to your liking. Alternatively, they can be barbecued.

Serve.

Minced Beef Pie
Serves 2

2 cups cooked minced beef curry with peas (see page 51)
1 sheet of butter puff pastry
2 tbsp chopped fresh coriander
1 egg

In a bowl, beat the egg and keep aside. In 2 individual pie dishes, add the minced beef curry then sprinkle coriander over the top. Cut pastry to fit as lids for the 2 pie dishes. Place these onto the pie dishes, covering the mince curry. Secure the ends by pinching together. Brush the top of the pastry with the beaten egg. Bake in the oven at 180°C for 30 minutes, until the pie is brown all over and thoroughly cooked.

Serve with potatoes of choice.

Steak with Chilli Sauce
Serves 2

2 steaks
¼ cup chilli sauce
1 tsp ginger and garlic paste (see page 91)

In a saucepan, add chilli sauce, ginger and garlic paste with ¼ cup of water. Bring to the boil and simmer gently, stirring until the mixture thickens and the water evaporates to leave a thick sauce. Heat a little oil in a frying pan and cook the steaks to your liking. Remove onto a plate and drizzle the chilli sauce on top.

Serve.

Steak with Orange Marinade
Serves 2

2 steaks
½ cup orange juice
1 tsp garam masala
1 tbsp chilli sauce

In a bowl, mix the orange juice and garam masala with chilli sauce, and season with salt. Add the steaks and coat with the marinade. Cover and leave for 1 hour. Grill or pan fry the steaks to your liking.

Serve.

Spicy Fillet Steak
Serves 2

2 steaks
2 tsp cumin seeds
1 tsp chilli flakes
¼ tsp garlic paste

In a frying pan, dry roast the cumin seeds until they release their aroma and change colour. Crush them in a pestle and mortar. Place in a bowl with garlic, chilli flakes and season with salt. Add 1 tbsp of oil and mix to a paste. Brush this paste over the steaks and grill, barbecue or fry the steaks to your liking.

Serve with a salad.

Tamarind Chilli Beef
Serves 2

250g beef, sliced into thin strips
2 tbsp tamarind paste
1 tbsp cumin seeds
2 tbsp lime juice

In a cup, mix the tamarind paste with ½ cup of water and keep aside. In a deep frying pan or wok, heat 2 tbsp of oil, add the cumin seeds and cook until they change colour. Add the beef, season with salt and chilli flakes. Stir fry until the beef is cooked and crispy. Add the tamarind paste mixture and stir fry for a further 2 minutes until no liquid is left. Stir in the lime juice. Remove onto a plate.

Serve with vegetables.

Indian Beef Burgers

Serves 4

500g minced beef
1 onion diced
1 bunch of chopped fresh coriander
½ jar madras curry paste

In a bowl, mix the mince with the chopped onion, curry paste and coriander, cover and leave in the fridge for about 1 hour. Shape the mince into burgers. Heat 2 tbsp of oil in a pan and cook the burgers until the meat is cooked, turning the burgers over. Alternatively, they can be barbecued.

Serve in a bun topped with raita, mango chutney and salad leaves.

Chilli Steak

Serves 4

4 beef steaks
1 lemon
1 tsp garam masala

Grate the rind from one lemon, preserving the juice. In a bowl, mix in the lemon rind, lemon juice and garam masala with 2 tbsp oil, season with salt and chilli flakes. Add the steaks and coat with the marinade. Cover and leave in the fridge for 2 hours. Grill steaks to your liking.

Serve with lemon wedges.

Beef with Chilli Butter
Serves 4

4 beef fillets
½ cup melted chilli butter (see page 92)

In a frying pan, melt the chilli butter, season with salt add the steaks and cook the beef steaks to your liking. Remove onto a plate.

Serve.

Crumbed Beef with Chilli Butter
Serves 4

4 beef fillets
1 cup breadcrumbs
2 tbsp chopped fresh coriander
½ cup melted chilli butter (see page 92)

In a frying pan, melt the chilli butter, add the beef fillets and cook the beef to your liking. Remove onto a plate. In a bowl, mix the breadcrumbs with coriander, season with salt and chilli flakes to taste. Sprinkle the fillets with the breadcrumbs and place under a grill. Cook until the breadcrumbs turn a golden brown in colour.

Serve.

Oysters with Mango and Chilli

Serves 2

8 oysters in shells
½ mango, diced finely
Lime juice

Take the oysters out of their shells and wash them. Place half the shells on a plate and put the washed oysters back into the shells. Top with mango cubes and drizzle with lime juice.

Serve.

Almond Fish

Serves 4

4 white fish fillets
1 cup ground almonds
1 tsp garam masala
1 egg

In a small bowl, mix ground almond with garam masala, season with salt and chilli flakes. In another bowl, beat the egg. Dip the fish first into the egg then coat in almond mixture. Place onto a greased baking tray. Cook in an oven at 180°C for 30 minutes, turning once. Remove onto a plate.

Serve with lemon wedges.

Ginger Soy Fish

Serves 4

4 white fish fillets
1 cup ginger and soy marinade
1 tbsp fresh coriander
1 tbsp grated ginger

Marinate the fish in a mixture of grated ginger and soya for 1 hour. Heat 2 tbsp oil in a frying pan, add the fish with the marinade sauce and ½ cup water. Bring to the boil, lower heat and simmer gently. Cook until the water has evaporated and the fish is cooked. Stir gently often so as not to break the fish. Remove onto a plate.

Serve sprinkled with coriander.

Crab and Pasta

Serves 4

200g crab meat, cooked
300g penne pasta
1 jar of tomato and chilli sauce
1 tsp cumin seeds

Cook the pasta as per packet instructions, then drain and keep aside. In a frying pan, heat 2 tbsp of oil, add the cumin seeds. When the seeds change colour, add the tomato and chilli sauce and season with salt, add 4 tbsp of water. Bring to the boil and keep stirring, simmer until the water has evaporated and the sauce thickens. Stir in the crab meat, with another 4 tbsp of water and cook for 5 minutes, until the crab meat is cooked and water evaporated. Add the pasta to the sauce and stir once.

Serve.

Salmon and Potato Cakes
Serves 4

2 cups mashed potatoes
400g canned salmon, drained and flaked
½ cup chopped fresh coriander leaves
1 tsp curry powder

In a bowl, mix all the ingredients together, season with salt and chilli flakes. Shape into 4 round patties. Heat 2 tbsp oil in a frying pan, and cook the salmon cakes until browned.

Serve with salad.

Marinated King Prawns
Serves 4

500g king prawns
3 tbsp tandoori tikka paste
½ cup plain yoghurt
Juice of 1 lemon

In a bowl, mix the tandoori paste with plain yoghurt and lemon juice. Add the prawns, ensuring they are coated. Leave to marinate in fridge for 2 hours or longer if possible. Grill or barbecue the prawns, brushing occasionally with the marinade.

Serve with lemon wedges.

Mustard Prawn Curry

Serves 4

500g king prawns
1 tbsp mustard seeds
1 tsp curry powder
1 onion, diced

In a bowl, cover the mustard seeds with boiling water. Stand for 10 minutes then strain. In a frying pan, heat 2 tbsp oil and cook the onions until golden brown. Add the curry powder and mustard seeds with some water. Bring to the boil, lower the heat and simmer until the water has evaporated and a thick sauce remains. Remove the sauce from the heat, and then blend the mixture until smooth. Return the mixture to the pan, add the prawns and cook until tender.

Serve with lemon wedges.

Fish with Pickling Spice

Serves 4

4 white fish fillets (any white fish will do)
2 tsp pickling spice, crushed roughly
1 lime

Grate the zest of one lime, preserving the juice. In a bowl, mix 2 tbsp oil, roughly crushed pickling spice, the lime rind and juice, season with salt and chilli flakes. Add the fish fillets and coat each fillet with the mixture. Leave to marinate for 1 hour. Grill the fish fillets on each side until cooked through.

Serve with lemon wedges.

Fish with Orange and Tamarind
Serves 4

4 white fish fillets
2 tbsp orange marmalade
2 tbsp tamarind paste
2 tbsp fresh ginger, cut into thin slices

In a bowl, mix the orange marmalade, tamarind paste, ginger and 2 tbsp oil, season with salt and chilli flakes. Add the fish fillets and coat fish on both sides, then marinate for 1 hour. Heat 2 tbsp oil in a frying pan; add the fish with the marinade. Cook on a low heat until the fish is cooked through, turn and cook the other side. Remove onto a plate.

Serve with lemon and orange wedges.

Spicy and Tangy Fried Fish
Serves 4

4 white fish fillets
1 tsp curry powder
1 tsp chaat masala
½ cup semolina

In a bowl, mix the curry powder and chaat masala with 2 tbsp oil, season with salt and chilli flakes. Add the fish fillets, coat with the mixture and marinate for 30 minutes. Place the semolina onto a plate. Take the fillets out of the marinade and coat with the semolina. Heat 4 tbsp oil in a deep frying pan; add the coated fillets to the pan. Fry until the fish is cooked and has turned golden brown. Remove onto kitchen paper to drain.

Serve with lemon wedges.

Tandoori Salmon

Serves 2

2 salmon fillets
2 tbsp tandoori curry paste
4 tbsp plain yoghurt

In a small bowl, mix the tandoori curry paste with the yoghurt. Add the salmon and cover with the paste mixture. Place in fridge for about 1 hour to marinate. Meanwhile, heat the oven to 180°C. Place the salmon onto a greased oven tray and bake in the oven for 30 minutes or longer depending on the thickness of the salmon fillets, until cooked.

Serve with a green salad.

Pickled salmon

Serves 2

2 salmon fillets
4 tbsp lime pickle

On a plate, arrange the salmon fillets skin side down. Spread lime pickle onto the fillets. In a small frying pan, add enough olive oil just to cover the bottom of the pan. Place the salmon fillets skin side down in the pan and cook on a slow heat, ensuring it does not burn. Cook until one side is cooked, then turn over with a spatula and cook the other side, ensuring the lime pickle stays underneath the salmon. If it moves, just place it back on top. Ensure the salmon is cook thoroughly.

Serve with a green salad and tamarind chutney.
Optional: The salmon may be cut into bite-size pieces and placed onto a plate with toothpicks to make a great party food.

Salmon with a Crust
Serves 2

2 small salmon fillets
2 tbsp tandoori paste
50g breadcrumbs
1 tbsp lemon juice

In a bowl, mix the breadcrumbs, tandoori paste and lemon juice. Spread the mixture over the top of the salmon, and lightly season with salt and chilli flakes. Bake in the oven at 180°C for 30 minutes until cooked.

Serve.

Salmon Fish Cakes
Serves 4

400g canned salmon, drained
1 lime
1 egg
50g breadcrumbs

Grate zest of one lime, preserving the juice. In a bowl, mix the salmon, lime zest and juice with 1 egg and breadcrumbs, season with salt and chilli flakes to taste. Combine all the ingredients and shape into round patties. Heat a little oil in a pan and fry the fish cakes until cooked, turning over.

Serve with a green salad.

Fish with Turmeric
Serves 2

2 firm white fish steaks, cod or halibut
½ tsp turmeric powder
½ tsp coriander powder

In a small bowl, mix the coriander powder and turmeric together. Rub over the fish steaks, ensuring they are covered well. Use a few drops of oil if the fish is not wet enough for the mixture to stick, season with salt and chilli flakes. Heat a little oil in a frying pan and add the fish steaks and cook one side first on a low heat until cooked through. Turn over and cook the other side.

Serve.

Fenugreek / Methi Salmon
Serves 2

2 salmon fillets
1 tbsp dried fenugreek leaves
2 tbsp tandoori paste
100 ml plain yoghurt

In a bowl, mix the tandoori paste with the yoghurt and fenugreek leaves, season with salt and chilli flakes. Place the salmon into the marinade and ensure it is evenly coated, leave for about 1 hour. Heat a little oil in a frying pan, and place the salmon into the pan with some of the marinade. Cook over a low heat until one side is cooked, then turn over and cook the other side.

Serve.

Mussels
Serves 4

500g of mussels
1 onion, diced
200 ml coconut milk
½ tsp turmeric powder

In a jug, mix together coconut milk and turmeric with 200ml of water, season with salt and chilli flakes, then keep aside. Heat 2 tbsp oil in a frying pan and cook the onions until golden brown in colour. Pour in the coconut mixture, and bring the mixture to boil. Add the mussels, then lower heat and simmer gently for 20 minutes, stirring often. When the mixture has reduced, remove from the heat. Discard any mussels that have not opened.

Serve with chopped coriander and chopped tomato.
Optional: Add 1 tbsp of ginger with the onions.

Prawn Curry
Serves 2

12 prawns
1 cup coconut milk
2 tbsp curry paste
1 lime

Grate zest of one lime, preserving the juice. In a frying pan, heat 1 tbsp of oil, add the prawns. Gently cook for about 2 minutes to seal the prawns. Add the curry paste, coconut milk and ½ cup of water. Bring to the boil, stirring all the time, then lower heat and simmer gently until the prawns are cooked, and a thick sauce remains. Add the lime zest and 2 tbsp of lime juice, then bring to boil again, stirring gently for 2 minutes. Remove from heat.

Serve with rice.

Vegetarian

Paneer Recipe

2 litres whole milk
6 tbsp lemon juice

Place a muslin cloth over a colander and keep aside. In a heavy bottomed pan, heat the milk until it reaches boiling point. Add the lemon juice whilst stirring all the time. The milk will curdle. Stir until the milk has curdled and there is a residue of whey. Do not stir too much as this may break up the paneer. Drain the paneer into the colander, ensuring that the milk solids remain in the muslin cloth. Tie the cloth and try to squeeze out as much liquid as possible. Be careful, as it will be hot. Secure the muslin cloth and place onto a draining board. Balance a heavy saucepan filled with water over the cloth to drain it. Leave to drain overnight. Use as required.

This will make approximately 200g. Use as required.

Paprika Baked Paneer
Serves 2

200g paneer, cut into slices (see above)
Handful of fresh coriander leaves
1 tsp paprika powder

Brush the paneer on both sides with oil and place the paneer onto a baking tray. Sprinkle with paprika and coriander leaves, season with salt and chilli flakes. Bake in the oven for 30 minutes at 180°C until the paneer is cooked and has turned a golden brown colour.

Serve with a chutney of your choice.

Cumin Potatoes
Serves 2

2 tsp cumin powder
2 potatoes, peeled and cut into cubes
1 tsp garam masala
2 tsp mango powder

In a frying pan, heat 1 tbsp of olive oil, then add the cumin seeds and fry until fragrant for approximately 30 seconds. Add the cubed potatoes, garam masala, season with salt and chilli flakes to taste. Add ½ cup water and stir. Bring to the boil, then lower heat and simmer until the potatoes are cooked and the water has evaporated, stir occasionally to prevent potatoes sticking to the pan. Add the mango powder and stir. Remove from heat

Serve as a side dish with a curry.

Baked Bean Curry
Serves 2

415g tin of baked beans
½ onion, chopped
1 tbsp curry powder
1 tsp garam masala

In a frying pan, heat 2 tbsp of oil, add the onions and cook until golden brown in colour. Add the baked beans and curry powder, season with salt and chilli flakes, add ¼ cup of water. Bring to boil, then lower heat and cook for about 5 minutes, stirring often until the water has evaporated. Add the garam masala and stir for a further 2 minutes.

Serve.

Scrambled Paneer

Serves 2

200g paneer, grated (see page 80)
1 onion, diced
1 tsp garam masala
1 tsp curry powder

In a frying pan, heat 2 tbsp of oil, add the onions and cook until browned. Mix in the grated paneer, curry powder and garam masala, season with salt and chilli flakes. Add ¼ cup of water. Cook until the water has completely evaporated and the mixture looks like scrambled eggs.

Serve sprinkled with coriander leaves.

Paneer Curry

Serves 2

200g paneer, cut into small cubes (see page 80)
1 tbsp curry paste
½ onion, diced
200g tinned chopped tomatoes

Heat a 2 tbsp of oil in a frying pan, then fry the paneer cubes until they have changed colour to a golden brown. Remove onto a plate and keep aside. In another saucepan, heat 1 tbsp of oil add the onions and cook until browned. Add the curry paste and stir for a few seconds to release the flavours. Add the tomatoes and cook for about 1 minute stirring, add the paneer cubes and ¼ cup water, season with salt and chilli flakes and bring to boil. Lower the heat and simmer gently until the water has evaporated to leave a thick sauce.

Serve with coriander as garnish.
Optional: Add frozen or fresh peas to the paneer to make mattar paneer.

Crispy Okra

Serves 2

150g okra
2 tsp cumin powder
2 tsp mango powder
2 tsp coriander powder

Wash the okra and dry thoroughly using a tea towel because it gets slimy when wet. Cut the okra into small rounds. Heat 3 tbsp of oil in a frying pan add the okra and all the spices, season with salt and chilli flakes. Cook for 20 minutes. Keep stirring until the okra is cooked and crispy.

Serve.

Cauliflower

Serves 2

1 small cauliflower, cut into small florets
1 onion, finely chopped
1 tsp garam masala
2 tsp curry powder

In a frying pan, heat 2 tbsp of oil, add the onion and cook until browned. Add the cauliflower, curry powder and garam masala, season with salt and chilli flakes to taste. Add ¼ cup of water and stir. Lower the heat and simmer gently until the water has evaporated completely and the cauliflower is cooked. Stir occasionally but make sure the cauliflower does not break up when stirring.

Serve with a coriander garnish.

Mashed Potatoes
Serves 2

2 potatoes
1 tbsp coriander leaves
½ onion, chopped finely
1 tsp cumin powder

Boil the potatoes and mash with a masher. Then mix in the coriander, onion, cumin powder and season with salt and chilli flakes.

Serve.

Potatoes with Fenugreek (aloo methi)
Serves 2

2 potatoes, skinned, boiled and cubed
1 onion, chopped
3 tbsp dried fenugreek leaves / kasoori methi
1 tsp curry powder

In a frying pan, heat 2 tbsp oil and add the chopped onions and cook until they turn brown. Add the potatoes and season with salt and chilli flakes. Stir to combine. Add the fenugreek leaves and curry powder with ½ cup water. Stir and bring to the boil then lower the heat and simmer until the water has evaporated and the potatoes are cooked, stirring occasionally. If the mixture is too dry, add a splash of water. Give it a final stir and remove from heat.

Serve.

Curried Dry Potatoes
Serves 4

4 potatoes, boiled and cut into cubes
½ tsp garam masala
½ tsp curry powder
1 tsp mango powder

In a frying pan heat 1 tbsp of oil, add the curry powder and garam masala. Cook for about 1 minute, stirring continually. Add the cubes of boiled potatoes with 2 tbsp of water, mix to coat in the spice, add mango powder and season with salt and chilli flakes. Cook until the potatoes are thoroughly cooked and soft but not mashed.

Serve with dosas or as a side dish.

Stuffed Mushrooms
Serves 4

4 large mushrooms
1 cup breadcrumbs
1 egg
2 tbsp dried fenugreek leaves / kasoori methi

Prepare the mushrooms by removing the outer skin and taking the middle stalks out. Place the mushrooms onto a baking dish and drizzle with oil. Beat the egg in a bowl and keep aside. In a frying pan, add 2 tbsp of oil then fry the breadcrumbs for 2 minutes. Add the fenugreek leaves, season with salt and chilli flakes, and cook until the breadcrumbs are a golden brown colour. Remove from heat and allow to cool. Mix in the beaten egg. Divide a quarter of the mixture onto each mushroom cap and bake in the oven for 20 minutes at 180°C or until the breadcrumbs are brown and the mushrooms have cooked.

Serve.

Pineapple Curry

Serves 4

1 fresh pineapple, cut into bite-size pieces (or 400g tinned pineapple chunks in
   their own juice)
1 tsp cumin seeds
2 tbsp curry powder
1 tsp brown sugar

In a frying pan, heat 1 tbsp of oil, add the cumin seeds and stir fry for about 1
minute until the seeds change colour. Add the curry powder and cook for 1
minute. Add the pineapple pieces and the juice from the fruit, season with salt and
chilli flakes to taste. Add the brown sugar and bring to boil. Reduce heat and stir
fry until the juice has evaporated and the pineapple caramelizes which should take
between 5 and 10 minutes.

Serve with naan bread.

French Green Beans

Serves 4

2 cups French green beans
1 tsp cumin seeds
½ tsp garam masala
1 tsp curry powder

In a frying pan, heat 1 tbsp oil, add the cumin seeds and fry until they turn dark
brown. Add the French beans and curry powder, season with salt and chilli flakes.
Add ¼ cup water and bring to the boil. Lower the heat and simmer gently until
cooked, stirring occasionally. Cook until the beans are tender. If the mixture is too
dry add just a little more water. Add garam masala and give it another stir.

Serve as a side dish to a curry.

White Cabbage
Serves 4

1 small white cabbage, cut finely
1 tsp mustard seeds
2 tsp curry powder
1 tsp garam masala

In a frying pan, heat 2 tbsp oil, add the mustard seeds and fry until they pop. Add the cabbage, curry powder and garam masala, season with salt and chilli flakes, stirring continually for about 2 minutes. Lower heat and simmer until the cabbage has cooked, stirring occasionally.

Serve as a side dish.

Potatoes and Mango Chutney
Serves 4

4 potatoes, diced
2 tbsp mango chutney
1 onion, chopped finely
½ tsp turmeric

In a saucepan, add 1 tbsp of oil and fry the onions until browned. Add the potatoes, turmeric and mango chutney, season with salt and chilli flakes. Stir in ½ cup of water and bring to the boil, lower heat and simmer until the water has evaporated and potatoes are tender but not falling apart.

Serve garnished with coriander as a side dish.

Indian Roast Potatoes
Serves 4

6 potatoes, peeled and par boiled
1 heaped tbsp curry powder

In a bowl mix 4 tbsp of oil with the curry powder. In a roasting dish, add the potatoes, Pour over the oil mixture and mix, ensuring the potatoes are fully coated. Roast the potatoes in the oven at 180°C for 45 minutes, until crispy and golden brown.

Serve.

Cauliflower and Potato (gobi aloo)
Serves 4

1 small cauliflower, cut into small pieces
2 potatoes, diced into the same size chunks as the cauliflower
2 tsp curry powder
1 onion, finely chopped

In a saucepan, heat 2 tbsp of oil and fry the onions until they are golden brown. Mix in the cauliflower and potatoes, along with the curry powder and season with salt and chilli flakes. Add ½ cup water and bring to boil. Lower heat and simmer until the cauliflower and potatoes are tender and the water has evaporated. If the pan becomes dry, add a little more water. Remove from heat.

Serve with coriander as a garnish.

Spiced Corn Cobs
Serves 4

4 sweetcorn cobs, with husks
1 tsp cumin seeds, toasted
Handful of fresh coriander leaves
4 tbsp butter

Tear out the silky threads from the corn and place the sweetcorn cobs in a bowl of water to soak for 5 minutes. In a frying pan, add the cumin seeds and dry roast until they change colour. Melt the butter in a bowl and mix with dry roasted cumin seeds and coriander leaves, season with salt and chilli flakes. Take the corn out of the water and place onto a grill and cook, turning until they have browned and are tender. Alternatively, the corn cobs can be barbecued. Once cooked, peel back the husks and brush with the spiced butter.

Serve warm; perfect as side to a barbecue.

Sweet Corn Masala
Serves 4

150g tinned sweetcorn
1 tsp cumin seeds
1 tsp curry powder
1 tsp mango powder

In a frying pan, heat 1 tbsp oil, add the cumin seeds and cook until they turn brown and release their flavour. Add the sweetcorn and curry powder, season with salt and chilli flakes to taste. Add ¼ cup water, and bring to the boil, then lower heat and simmer for 20 minutes until the corn is tender and the water has evaporated. Stir in the mango powder and cook for a further 1 minute. Remove from heat.

Serve.

Romano Peppers with Paneer

Serves 4

4 romano peppers
2 tbsp curry paste
200g paneer, diced (see page 80)
Handful of fresh coriander leaves

Pre-heat the oven at 180°C. In a frying pan, heat the curry paste and add the diced paneer with ¼ cup water. Stir and cook until the water has evaporated. Stir the coriander leaves into the paneer mixture. Slice the romano peppers lengthwise and remove the seeds. Brush them with oil and place onto a baking tray and bake in the oven for 5 minutes each side. Fill each romano pepper with the paneer mixture and place back into the oven. Cook for a further 5 minutes.

Serve.

Peppers Stuffed With Potatoes

Serves 4

4 green peppers
2 tbsp curry paste
3 potatoes, diced
Handful of coriander leaves

Pre-heat the oven at 180°C. In a saucepan, heat the curry paste and add the diced potatoes, season with salt and chilli flakes and add ¼ cup of water. Stir and cook until the water has evaporated and the potatoes are tender. Stir the coriander leaves into the potatoes. Slice the tops of the peppers and keep aside, scoop out the middle and seeds and discard. Brush with oil and place onto a baking tray and bake in the oven for 5 minutes. Fill each pepper with the potato mixture and place back into the oven. Cook for a further 5 minutes. Place the reserved tops onto the peppers before serving.

Serve.

Indian style cheese and chilli toast
Serves 2

4 slices of white bread
1 cup grated cheddar cheese
2 tomatoes chopped
1 -2 green chillies chopped into small rounds

In a bowl add the cheese, chopped tomatoes and chopped green chilli, season with salt.

Place the sliced bread under a grill and brown, take out on to a plate and turn over, sprinkle the cheese mixture evenly over the side of bread not toasted and place under the grill again. Cook until the cheese has melted and small brown spots appear on the surface. Remove onto a plate and cut each slice into two diagonally.

Serve.

Marinades and Pastes

Ginger and Garlic Paste

½ cup fresh ginger skin removed
½ cup garlic cloves, skinned
¼ cup oil

Place all the ingredients into a blender and blend to a smooth paste. Store the paste in the fridge and use in curries or freeze in small quantities and use as and when required.

Chilli Butter

Serves 4

½ cup melted butter
¼ cup coriander paste
2 fresh green chillis, chopped finely

In a bowl, mix all the ingredients together. Store the butter in the fridge and use as required.

Chilli Garlic sauce

Serves 4

4 tbsp chilli sauce
2 tsp garlic paste

In a bowl, mix all the ingredients together. Store the sauce in the fridge and use as required.

Garam Masala

'Garam' means hot and 'masala' means a mixture of spices in Indian. The heat referred to by garam is not chilli heat, but the kind of heat supplied by spices. The various regions in India and commercial brands will all have different spices mixed together in their versions of garam masala. Thus, there is not one recipe for garam masala. Here is a very easy simple recipe using just four spices.

1 tsp black pepper
1 tsp cloves
4 black cardamons
1 inch cinnamon stick

Dry roast the ingredients and grind to a powder. Store the gram masala in an airtight jars and use as required.

Indian Curries

The word 'curry' is used to describe Indian cuisine as a whole and yet curry is not even an Indian word. In reality, it is an anglicised word of an Indian term used primarily outside of India. Many believe that curry may have been derived from 'kari', a South Indian word used to describe a leaf ingredient used in cooking with a sauce. Ironically, restaurants in large Indian cities such as Mumbai, New Delhi and Bangalore now use the word curry to appeal to Western visitors.

In Indian households a dish is described as being either 'sukhi' (dry) or 'tari' (wet). These are the terms I am familiar with, and my mother still uses them. Curries are what we would call wet dishes. In the west, especially in the UK, curries have been given names that originated in the UK. Some of the names for curries are not heard of in India and people do not know what they mean. These are entirely new dishes created in the west.

The essential ingredients of an Indian curry are onions, garlic and ginger (as stated by the UK Food Standards Agency). Seasoned with salt and chilli, this forms the base of the dish, after which spices and tomatoes are added. My recipes for different curries use these base ingredients and then add in four ingredients to develop a distinct dish. The method is easy, quick and uses the minimum of ingredients needed to create a curry. Knowing the basics will allow you, when you have time to experiment, to eventually adapt the recipes and cook curries to your own individual taste.

To save time, ginger and garlic pastes can be bought individually and then mixed in equal measures to form a ginger and garlic paste, which can be stored in the fridge in airtight containers. In some recipes, to make them easier, I have used curry paste which substitutes some of the ingredients. However, this in no way distorts the flavours. It must be noted that curry powder is not a spice, nor is it from India, but it is a blend of different spices used to create curries outside of India. Different brands of curry powder will have different ingredients, so I suggest that you familiarise yourself with a few varieties to find the one that most suits your tastes.

Basic Masala Sauce Recipe

Having a masala sauce to hand saves time. To this, any meats or vegetables can be added, along with other spices and herbs, to create quick and easy dishes in little time.

Basic Masala Sauce Recipe

2 onions, finely chopped and blended to a paste
2 tsp ginger and garlic paste (see page 91)
400g tinned chopped tomatoes
½ jar curry paste

In a saucepan, heat 3 tbsp oil, then fry the finely blended onions, along with the ginger and garlic paste. Cook until the onions brown, stirring continually so that the mixture does not stick to the bottom of the pan. When the onions have browned, add the chopped tomatoes, the curry paste, season with salt and chilli flakes, and cook for about a minute whilst stirring. Add 1 cup of water stir and bring to the boil. Lower the heat and cook until the water has evaporated and a thick sauce remains.

Use this sauce as a base for curries. This masala sauce can be stored in glass containers or frozen to be used as required.

Chicken Tikka Masala

This dish was devised in Britain in early 1960s to appeal to the English palate. In India, chicken tikka is dry, but the British preferred a dish with gravy. So a masala was created to accompany the chicken tikka.

Chicken Tikka Masala
Serves 4

1 onion, finely chopped
1 tsp ginger and garlic paste (see page 91)

500g chicken, cut into cubes
3 tbsp tandoori tikka paste
200g tinned chopped tomatoes puréed
1 cup yoghurt

In a deep frying pan, heat 1 tbsp oil then mix in 2 tbsp of the tikka paste and 2 tbsp of water. Cook for about 1 minute. Add the chicken pieces and mix to coat the chicken with the tikka paste. Add ¼ cup water and bring to the boil. Lower the heat and simmer until the chicken is cooked, stirring all the time. Remove and keep aside.

In a saucepan, add 2 tbsp of oil and fry the onions, ginger and garlic paste until the onions turn a golden brown colour, stirring continually to ensure they do not burn. Add the tomatoes and 1 tbsp of tikka paste, season with salt and chilli flakes, then add ¼ cup of water. Whilst stirring, cook until the water has evaporated and a thick sauce remains. Mix in the cooked chicken tikka pieces, and then add the yoghurt, whilst stirring. When the yoghurt has been incorporated, add ¼ cup water and bring to the boil. Lower the heat and whilst stirring cook until there is a thick sauce left and the water has evaporated. If the sauce is too watery, boil further to evaporate the water. If too dry, add more water a little at a time.

Serve with rice and naan bread, with sprinkled coriander as garnish.
Optional: Replace the yoghurt with cream to give a much richer sauce.

Butter Chicken / Murgh Makhani

Butter chicken has its origin in Punjab and it is a dish commonly associated with the Sikh community. It first appeared in a restaurant called Moti Mahal in New Delhi in 1947, shortly after the partition of India. The dish is cooked in butter, hence its name, with the addition of dried fenugreek leaves to give it a distinct flavour.

I have used olive oil in this recipe. In no way does this detract from the flavour, but you may wish to replace the oil with ghee.

Butter Chicken (murgh makhani)
Serves 4

1 onion, minced to a paste
1 tsp ginger and garlic paste (see page 91)

2 skinless chicken breast, diced into bite size pieces
3 tbsp tandoori paste
2 tbsp tomato paste
2 tbsp dried fenugreek leaves / kasoori methi

In a bowl add 2 tbsp tandoori paste, add the chicken pieces and mix to coat, marinate in the fridge for 2 hours or longer if possible. In a blender, blend the onion and the ginger and garlic paste with 2 tbsp of water. If more water is needed, just add a little at a time. It should not be runny, but a thick paste consistency. Pour this into a saucepan with 2 tbsp of heated oil. Cook until the onions have browned and water has evaporated, stirring continually. Add 1 tbsp tandoori paste and 2 tbsp tomato paste, season with salt and chilli flakes and add ¼ cup water. Cook until the water has evaporated and the mixture comes to a sauce consistency. You will see the oil separating in the pan from the mixture. Add the marinated tandoori chicken pieces and ½ cup of water. Bring to the boil, lower the heat and simmer until the water has evaporated and the chicken is cooked in a thick sauce, stir often. Stir in the fenugreek leaves and cook for a further 5 minutes. Remove.

Serve with rice and naan breads, sprinkled with coriander as garnish.

Beef Madras

Madras curry is a hot curry with a sauce which uses lots of chilli powder to get the red colour. It originated in the south of India and gets its name from the city of Madras during the time of British rule in India. The city is now known as Chennai.

An authentic madras curry is vegetarian, but here it is adapted into a meat dish.

Beef Madras
Serves 4

1 onion, finely chopped
1 tsp ginger and garlic paste (see page 91)

500g beef, cut into cubes
2 tbsp madras curry paste
200g tinned chopped tomatoes
3 tbsp mango chutney

In a saucepan, heat 2 tbsp of oil then add the chopped onions, ginger and garlic paste and cook until browned. Add the curry paste, chopped tomatoes, ¼ cup of water, season with salt and chilli flakes. Bring to the boil, stirring all the time until the water has evaporated. Add the beef cubes with 1 cup water, and bring to the boil again. Lower the heat and simmer gently until the sauce thickens and the meat is tender, stirring often. Stir in the mango chutney and bring to the boil again. Remove from heat.

Serve sprinkled with coriander as a garnish.

Balti Chicken

Balti literally translates as 'bucket' in Indian. It is served in a type of small wok made of cast iron, hence the name. The balti curry has its origins in Birmingham in the UK in the early 1990s and is now a popular item on restaurant menus nationwide. It is not a dish traditionally cooked or served in India. However, it is now appearing on some restaurant menus in the major Indian cities.

Balti Chicken
Serves 4

1 onion, finely chopped
1 tsp ginger and garlic paste (see page 91)

2 chicken breasts, cut into cubes
2 tbsp balti curry paste
2 tsp cumin seeds
200g tinned chopped tomatoes

In a saucepan heat 2 tbsp oil and add cumin seeds and cook until they change to a golden brown colour. Add the onions with the ginger and garlic paste and cook until the onions have turned a golden brown colour. Add the balti paste and tomatoes with ¼ cup of water, season with salt and chilli flakes and cook until the water has evaporated and a thick sauce remains. Add the chicken pieces and 1 cup of water. Bring to a boil, then lower the heat and simmer gently until the chicken is cooked. Keep an eye on the curry and give it an occasional stir. If the curry becomes too dry, add more water. If the chicken is cooked and the sauce is watery, turn up the heat and boil until the right consistency of the sauce remains.

Serve sprinkled with coriander as a garnish.

Rogan Josh

Rogan josh is an aromatic curry from the Kashmir and Punjab regions of India and is popular in both India and the United Kingdom. 'Rogan' means oil and 'josh' means hot as in high temperature rather than chilli heat. Therefore rogan josh means a dish cooked in oil at an intense heat.

The red colour is essential to this dish and is achieved using kashmiri mirch, which means 'pepper from Kashmir'. This ground pepper is red in colour, but not as hot as grounded black peppercorns. The Punjab version differs from the Kashmir version in that it will contain onions and tomatoes, whereas the Kashmir version will not. An authentic rogan josh will be made using lamb. I have used onions and tomatoes in this recipe, since this is the most well-known version of rogan josh.

Rogan Josh Lamb
Serves 4

1 onion, finely chopped
1 tsp ginger and garlic paste (see page 91)

500g lamb, cut into cubes
2 tbsp kashmiri masala curry paste or rogan josh curry paste
1 cup plain yoghurt
200g tinned chopped tomatoes

In a saucepan, heat 2 tbsp oil then add the chopped onion, ginger and garlic paste, cook until the onions change colour. Add the curry paste and chopped tomatoes along with ¼ cup of water, season with salt and chilli flakes. Cook until the water has evaporated, stirring often. Add the lamb and 1 cup of water. Bring to the boil, then lower the heat and simmer gently until the lamb is cooked and the water has evaporated to a sauce, stir often. Add the yoghurt and keep stirring for another 2 minutes. Remove.

Serve with rice and naan breads, sprinkled with coriander as garnish.

Bhuna Chicken

Bhuna refers to the cooking process of this dish. It is a dry dish with very little gravy. Chicken is usually used and the dish may contain green peppers. Again, there are different versions of the dish and it does not necessarily have to be hot.

Bhuna Chicken
Serves 4

1 onion, finely chopped
1 tsp ginger and garlic paste (see page 91)

2 chicken breasts, with skin removed and cut into cubes
2 tbsp bhuna paste
200g tinned chopped tomatoes
2 green peppers cored and cut into large chunks

Place the chunks of pepper onto a tray and drizzle some oil over the top, place under a grill and chargrill the green peppers, turning over during cooking, keep aside. In a sauce pan, heat 2 tbsp oil then add the onions and the ginger and garlic paste. Cook until the onions change colour, add the bhuna paste and chopped tomatoes with ¼ cup of water. Cook until the water has evaporated, stirring often. Add the chicken and the chargrilled green peppers and 1 cup of water, season with salt and chilli flakes. Bring to the boil and then lower the heat. Simmer gently until the chicken is cooked and the water has evaporated to a sauce, stirring occasionally. Once the chicken is cooked, turn the heat up and cook for another 2 minutes, whilst stirring all the time. The bhuna process involves drying any liquid remaining in the dish, by stirring on a high heat.

Serve sprinkled with coriander as garnish, with rice and vegetables.

Jalfrezi

Jalfrezi is not an Indian dish, but one that was devised during the time of British rule in India. It is a method of cooking similar to stir frying. Leftover cooked meats or marinated meats and vegetables are generally used to create this dish. Restaurants in India rarely have jalfrezi on their menus, but the dish is a popular item in UK restaurants and invariably contains green peppers, onion and tomatoes. It can be quite a hot dish if more chillies are added to the dish.

Jalfrezi Chicken
Serves 4

2 onions: 1 chopped finely and 1 chopped in large chunks
1 tsp ginger and garlic paste (see page 91)

2 chicken breasts, with skin removed and cubed
3 tbsp jalfrezi paste
5 tomatoes: 2 chopped roughly and 3 chopped finely
2 roughly chopped green peppers

In a frying pan, heat 2 tbsp of oil, add 2 tbsp jalfrezi paste, and mix in the chicken with ¼ cup of water. Cook until the water has evaporated and chicken cooked, stirring continually, keep aside. In another pan, heat 2 tbsp oil then add the finely chopped onions and the ginger and garlic paste and cook until onions change colour. Then add the 3 finely chopped tomatoes, 1 tbsp jalfrezi paste, ¼ cup of water, season with salt and chilli flakes. Cook until the water has evaporated and a thick sauce remains, whilst stirring. Add the green peppers and cook for about 5 minutes to cook the peppers, whilst stirring often. Add the cooked chicken, along with the any remaining sauce, and ¼ cup water. Bring to the boil and then lower the heat and simmer, stirring to evaporate the water. Stir in the 2 roughly chopped tomatoes and the large chunks of chopped onion and cook, stirring for another 5 minutes. Remove from heat.

Serve sprinkled with coriander, and with rice and vegetables.
Optional: Add in 3 to 4 dried red chillies at the same time as the peppers.

Korma Chicken

Korma has its roots in the Mogul era in India. It is a mild creamy sauce, pale in colour and often has coconut cream and nuts added to the dish. It is quite a rich dish because of the cream and nuts. It is popular in the UK because it is mild.

Korma Chicken
Serves 4

1 onion, finely chopped
1 tsp ginger and garlic paste (see page 91)

2 chicken breasts, cut into cubes
3 tbsp korma paste
1 cup single cream
Handful of toasted slivered almonds

In a frying pan, add the almonds and dry fry them until they turn a golden brown colour. Remove and keep aside. In a saucepan, heat 2 tbsp oil then add the chopped onions and the ginger and garlic paste. Cook until the onions change colour, then add the korma paste and ¼ cup of water, season with salt and chilli flakes, stir continually, and cook until the water has evaporated and a thick sauce remains. Add the chicken with 1 cup water and bring to the boil. Lower the heat and simmer until the chicken is cooked, stir often. Once the chicken is cooked stir in the cream and keep stirring until the cream has been incorporated and a thick sauce remains. Throw in the toasted almonds and remove from heat.

Serve with rice and vegetables.
Optional: Throw in 4 dried red chillies just before removing from heat to give the curry a little colour.

Vindaloo

Vindaloo is derived from the Portuguese phrase 'Carne de Vinha d'Alhos': 'vinha' means wine or vinegar and 'alhos' means garlic. The dish was introduced by the Portuguese during their time in India and is chiefly popular in the Goa region of India. In India, spices were added to liven up the dish and the name vindaloo remains. An authentic vindaloo is made using pork and contains garlic and vinegar. It can be quite a hot dish with the plentiful use of chillies, but other versions can be fairly mild.

Vindaloo Pork
Serves 4

1 onion, blended to a paste
1 tsp ginger and garlic paste (see page 91)

500g lean pork, cut into cubes
½ jar vindaloo paste
¼ cup vinegar
4 dried red chillies

In a blender, blend the onions to a paste, using ¼ cup water. Ensure that the paste is not too runny. In a saucepan, heat 2 tbsp oil then add the blended onions with the ginger and garlic paste, add the vinegar, vindaloo paste and ¼ cup water, season with salt and chilli flakes. Whilst stirring, heat until all the water has evaporated and a thick sauce remains, the oil will start to separate from the mixture in the pan. Mix in the pork and add 1 cup water. Bring to the boil, stirring continually. Lower the heat and simmer until the pork is tender, stir often. Once the pork is cooked, turn up the heat to boil away any remaining liquid until a thick sauce remains. Throw in the dried red chillies and stir, remove from heat.

Serve with rice and vegetables.

South Indian Fish

The regions of Kerala, Tamil Nadu and Goa in the south of India are renowned for their fish dishes with spices and coconut. Rice is a staple diet item, rather than wheat chapatis, as is coconut and tamarind chutneys. These dishes primarily use pomfret fish which occur all along the coast of India and are particularly abundant in Mumbai and Gujarat regions of India.

Fish with Coconut and Tamarind
Serves 4

1 onion, finely chopped
1 tsp ginger and garlic paste (see page 91)

4 white fish steaks
2 tbsp tamarind paste
1½ cup coconut cream
2 tsp curry powder

In a frying pan, heat 2 tbsp oil then add the chopped onions, ginger and garlic paste and cook until the onions have browned. Mix in the curry powder and tamarind paste and cook until flavours are released, which should be about 2 minutes. Stir in the coconut cream and bring to the boil. Add in the fish steaks and simmer for about 10 minutes until the fish is cooked through and tender. Carefully turn the fish steaks during cooking, ensuring they don't break. When the fish is cooked remove from heat.

Serve.

Easy Fish Curry

Serves 4

1 onion, finely chopped
1 tsp ginger and garlic paste (see page 91)

4 white fish fillets (e.g. cod or similar)
2 tbsp curry paste
200g tinned chopped tomatoes

In a frying pan, heat 3 tbsp oil, add the onions, ginger and garlic paste and cook until the onions have browned. Add the tomatoes, with the curry paste season with salt and chilli flakes to taste and cook until flavours are released, which should be about 2 minutes. Add ½ cup water and stir, add the fish fillets. Stir gently careful not to break the fish and bring to boil. Lower heat and simmer gently shaking the pan to prevent the fish from breaking. Cook until the fish is cooked through and the water has evaporated to leave a thick sauce. Remove from heat.

Serve with rice and naan breads and sprinkled with fresh coriander.

Vegetarian

Chickpea Curry / Channa Masala
Serves 4

Chickpeas can be bought in a dried form or canned. If bought dried, they will need to be washed and soaked overnight. I have used chickpeas in a tin which are ready to use. Channa masala is essentially a curry and therefore onions, ginger and garlic have not been included with the four ingredients to complete the dish.

1 onion, finely chopped
1 tsp ginger and garlic paste (see page 91)

400g tinned chickpeas
2 tbsp madras curry paste
200g tinned tomatoes
2 tsp pomegranate powder

Empty the chickpeas into a colander and wash them, then keep aside. In a saucepan with a lid heat 2 tbsp of oil, then add the onions and the ginger and garlic paste. Cook until the onions turn brown. Add the tomatoes and the madras curry paste, season with salt and chilli flakes. Cook for about 5 minutes, stirring all the time to break up the tomatoes and form a paste. Add the chickpeas to the saucepan and 2 cups of water, and bring to the boil. Lower the heat and cover the saucepan, simmer for about 30 minutes until the water evaporates and forms a thick sauce and the chickpeas have softened further. Stir often. Once the chickpeas have cooked, stir in the ground pomegranate powder, then give the curry a final stir and bring to the boil once more. Remove from heat.

Serve sprinkled with coriander as a garnish.

Red Kidney Beans (raj ma)

Serves 4

Red kidney beans can be bought dried or canned. If bought dried, they will need to be washed and soaked overnight. I have used canned red kidney beans which are ready to use. This raj ma recipe is essentially a curry and therefore onion, ginger and garlic have not been included with the four ingredients to complete the dish.

1 onion, finely chopped
1 tsp ginger and garlic paste (see page 91)

400g tinned red kidney beans
200g tinned chopped tomatoes
1 tsp garam masala
½ cup single cream

Empty the kidney beans into a colander and wash them, then keep aside. In a saucepan with a lid heat 2 tbsp of oil then add the onions and the ginger and garlic paste. Cook until the onions turn brown. Add the tomatoes, season with salt and chilli flakes and cook for about 2 minutes, stirring all the time to breaking the tomatoes until a thick sauce forms. Add the kidney beans to the saucepan along with 2 cups of water, and bring to the boil. Lower the heat and cover the saucepan with a lid simmer for about 30 minutes until the water evaporates and forms a thick sauce and the kidney beans have softened further. Once they are cooked, stir in the cream and garam masala. Give the curry a final stir and bring to the the boil once more. Remove from heat.

Serve sprinkled with coriander as garnish.

Lentils / Dhal

In India lentils, legumes, are refered to as dhals and form an integral part of Indian cooking and make a terrific addition to your repertoire as they are healthy, full of protein and low in fat. Every region of India has their own speciality of dhals and different ways of cooking them. However, the primary method of cooking remains the same: lentils are essentially boiled in water to soften them and then a tarka, a blend of different spices and ingredients is added before serving. The result is always delicious.

Dhals can be served as a main dish or as a side dish, depending on your preference and the type of dhal. Bear in mind that some dhals take longer to prepare than others. The time the lentils take to soften usually depends on whether they are whole or split. I have shown the cooking method for different dhals using two ingredients. This forms the basic dhal which can be made in volume and frozen in individual portions. Then I have used four or less ingredients in the tarka. Having a basic recipe that can be developed in different ways will allow you to experiment and create dhals according to your own individual taste.

To assist you to recognise the individual varieties, I've included a list of dhals below with their Indian and English names.

Indian Name	English Name
Masoor dhal split	Red split lentils
Sabut masoor dhal	Brown lentils
Urad dhal or ma di dhal	Whole black lentils, also known as Makhani Dhal
Channa dhal	Split chickpeas, pale yellow in colour
Urad dhal white	White split lentils

Red Lentils (masoor dhal)
Serves 4

This is the easiest Dhal to cook.

1 cup red lentils
2 tsp curry powder

Wash the dhal in several changes of water, then place in a saucepan with a lid, add the curry powder. Add 2 cups of water to the pan and salt to taste, and bring to the boil. Lower the heat and cover pan and simmer for about 30 minutes. Keep an eye on the dhal to prevent it drying out or boiling over, and give it an occasional stir. If the water runs dry add some more, if there is too much water, this can be boiled off on a high heat. The dhal will be ready when it has thickened and the grains are soft but not mushy.
Apply tarka to the dhal before serving.

Tarka

2 tsp cumin seeds
1 tsp ginger and garlic paste (see page 91)
200g tinned chopped tomatoes

In a frying pan, heat 1 tbsp of oil, then add the cumin seeds and fry for about 1 minute until the seeds change colour. Add the ginger and garlic paste and cook for 1 minute. To this add the cooked dhal and stir to incorporate. Bring dhal to the boil, and then turn off the heat and leave to stand for 1 minute before serving.

Serve sprinkled with coriander as a garnish.

Brown Lentils (sabut masoor dhal)

Serves 4

1 cup brown lentils
1 tsp ginger and garlic paste (see page 91)

Wash the dhal in several changes of water, then place in a saucepan with a lid, add 2 cups water and the ginger and garlic paste. Bring to the boil, then cover the saucepan and lower the heat. Simmer for about 1 hour, keeping an eye on the dhal to prevent it drying out or boiling over, giving it an occasional stir. If the water runs dry, add some more, if there is too much water, this can be boiled off on a high heat. The dhal will be ready when it has thickened and the grains are soft but not mushy.
Apply tarka to the dhal before serving.

Tarka

1 onion, finely chopped
200g tinned chopped tomatoes
2 tbsp dried fenugreek leaves
1 tsp garam masala

In a frying pan, heat 2 tbsp of oil then add the onion and cook until browned. Add the chopped tomatoes and season with salt and chilli flakes to taste. Cook the tomatoes whilst stirring, which should take about 5 minutes. Then add the fenugreek leaves and cook for a further 2 minutes. To this add the cooked dhal and stir to combine. Stir in the the garam masala and bring the dhal to the boil. Turn off the heat, then leave to stand for 1 minute before serving.

Serve sprinkled with coriander as a garnish.

Black Lentils (makhani dhal)
Serves 4

Black dhal is whole grain of dhal and is quite tough. It is normally cooked in a pressure cooker to reduce the cooking time, but in this recipe I have boiled the dhal for 2 hours to soften.

1 cup black lentils
1 tsp of ginger and garlic paste (see page 91)

Wash the dhal in several changes of water, and place in a sauce pan with a lid, add 4 cups of water and the ginger and garlic paste. Stir and bring to the boil then cover the saucepan. Lower the heat and simmer for about 2 hours, keeping an eye on the dhal to prevent it drying out or boiling over, giving it an occasional stir. If the water runs dry add some more, if there is too much water, this can be boiled off on a high heat. The dhal will be ready when it has thickened and the grains are soft but not mushy.

Apply tarka to the dhal before serving.

Tarka

1 onion, finely chopped
200g tinned chopped tomatoes
1 tsp garam masala

In a frying pan, heat 2 tbsp of oil, then add the onion and cook until browned. Add the chopped tomatoes and season with salt and chilli flakes to taste. Cook until the tomatoes have been incorporated which should take about 5 minutes. Add the cooked dhal to the mixture with the garam masala and bring to the boil whilst stirring, and cook for a further 2 minutes stirring all the time. Remove from heat.

Serve sprinkled with coriander as a garnish.

Chickpea Lentils (channa dhal)
Serves 4

Channa dhal is split chickpeas and is not as hard as the black dhal, but still quite hard and needs to be softened. They are normally cooked in a pressure cooker to reduce the cooking time, but in this recipe I have boiled the dhal for 1 hour to soften.

1 cup channa lentils
Pinch of turmeric powder

Wash the dhal in several changes of water, then place in a saucepan with a lid add 4 cups of water and turmeric. Bring to the boil, and remove any scum that may have formed on the top in the saucepan. Lower the heat and cover the saucepan and simmer for about 1 hour, keeping an eye on the dhal to prevent it drying out or boiling over and giving it an occasional stir. If the water runs dry add some more, if there is too much water, this can be boiled off on a high heat. The dhal will be ready when it has thickened and the grains are soft but not mushy.

Apply tarka to the dhal before serving.

Tarka

2 tsp cumin seeds
1 tsp ginger and garlic paste (see page 91)
1 tbsp tamarind paste
1 tsp garam masala

In a frying pan, heat 2 tbsp of oil then add the cumin seeds and the ginger and garlic paste, cooking until the cumin seeds change colour. Add the tamarind paste and garam masala, and season with salt and chilli flakes to taste. Add 2 tbsp of water, stirring continually until the water has evaporated. Add the cooked dhal to this mixture and bring to the boil, stirring. Remove from heat.

Serve sprinkled with coriander as garnish.

Saag

A Punjabi speciality, saag is a dish made with green mustard leaves and spinach and served with plenty of butter and accompanied with makki ki roti, a chapati made with corn flour. Often you will find saag incorporated into a paneer or meat dish. The most well-known dishes are saag aloo, which is saag with potatoes.

However, in restaurants you can often find saag on its own too. This spinach-only dish is called 'palak' in Indian.

In this book I have shown the method for saag, I have cooked saag using spinach without green mustard leaves, since the latter is not widely available.

After the saag is cooked, a serving portion is taken from the pan, and a tarka is applied to the portion being served.

Saag is served with a spoonful of butter placed in the middle of the portion being served.

Saag
Serves 4

1 tin chopped spinach
2 tsp ginger and garlic paste (see page 91)
1 tbsp maize flour (if unavailable use polenta)
1 tsp curry powder

In a saucepan, add the chopped spinach with ginger and garlic paste and curry powder. Add ½ cup water and bring to the boil. Lower the heat and simmer gently until the water has evaporated. Cool the mixture a little and using a hand blender, blend the spinach to a thick paste, but not too finely. Return to the heat and add the flour with ¼ cup water, and bring to the boil. Lower the heat and simmer gently for another 15 minutes to cook the flour. If the saag is too thick, add more water to get the right consistency.
Apply tarka to the saag before serving.

Tarka

½ cup melted butter, plus extra when serving
1 onion, chopped finely

In a frying pan, heat the butter, add the onions, season with salt and chilli flakes and cook until the onions have turned brown. Add the cooked saag and stir. Remove from the heat into a bowl and add a dollop of butter in the middle just before serving.

Serve with makki di roti see page 143

Saag Aloo
Serves 4

1 tin chopped spinach
2 tsp ginger and garlic paste (see page 91)
1 tbsp maize flour (if unavailable, use polenta)
1 tsp curry powder

In a saucepan, add the chopped spinach with ginger and garlic paste and curry powder. Add ½ cup water and bring to the boil. Lower the heat and simmer gently until the water has evaporated. Cool the mixture a little and using a hand blender, blend the spinach to a thick paste, but not too finely. Return to the heat and add the flour with ¼ cup water, and bring to the boil. Lower the heat and simmer gently for another 15 minutes to cook the flour. If the saag is too thick, add more water to get the right consistency.
Apply tarka to the saag aloo before serving.

Tarka

½ cup melted butter, plus extra for serving
1 onion, finely chopped
2 potatoes, diced
1 tsp garam masala

In a frying pan, heat the butter, then add the onions and cook until the onions have turned brown. Add the diced potatoes along with the garam masala, season with salt and chilli flakes. Add ¼ cup water, and bring to the boil. Lower the heat and simmer until the potatoes are soft and cooked through, stirring often. Add more water if required, the potatoes should be tender but retain their shape. Add the cooked saag to the potatoes and cook for 1 minute, stirring continually. Remove from heat.

Serve with makki di roti (see page 143) and a dollop of butter

Dosa

To the British, dosas are somewhat reminiscent of pancakes or crêpes. Indigenous to Kerala and Tamil Nadu in the south of India, they are made using rice batter and lentils. They are a hugely adaptable dish, served as breakfast, lunch or dinner, even as a snack. Dosas are becoming increasingly popular on restaurant menus within the UK and although they can be a little tricky to make at home, they are well worth it.

Dosas can be served in a great variety of ways. They can be stuffed with different fillings such as potatoes, meats or fish. They can also be served with sauces or chutneys, particularly coconut chutney. Most commonly, there are served with a thin lentil dhal almost like a soup. There are many variations of the dosa itself, such as a sweet dosa with sugar or a butter dosa using butter instead of oil, to name just a couple.

Dosa
Serves 4

1 cup white urad dhal
2 cups long grain rice
¼ tsp fenugreek seeds

Wash the dhal and rice in several changes of water. Soak them in a large bowl with fenugreek seeds in 2 litres of water for 4 hours. Drain the dhal and place into a food processor and grind to a paste consistency. If the batter is too thick, add 2 tbsp of water at a time when needed. Place the batter into another large bowl, cover and leave to ferment in a warm place overnight (the kitchen top will do). The batter will rise and double in size, so the bowl needs to be able to accommodate the rise in the batter. After it has fermented, add salt to taste. The batter should have a thick consistency. If more water is required, just add another 1 tablespoon at a time to get it to the right consistency.

Heat an iron griddle pan or a frying pan until hot; add 1 tsp of oil to the pan and swirl to cover the bottom of the pan. Lower the heat to medium. Taking a large spoonful of the batter, pour into the hot pan, and with the back of the spoon, spread the mixture in a circular motion so that it forms a thin layer in the bottom of the pan. Leave to cook, the bottom of the dosa should be browned; it will take about 1 -2 minutes. Make sure the bottom side is cooked and there are no liquid spots on the top side, otherwise it will be difficult to turn over. Sprinkle a few drops of oil on the dosa and flip it over and leave to cook for another 1-2 minutes. When the dosa is cooked on both sides, remove onto a plate and fold in half. Continue until all the batter has been used up.

Serve hot with your choice of filling and coconut chutney.

Sauce for Dosa

Serves 4

1 onion
200g tinned chopped tomatoes
1 tsp sambar powder
½ tsp mustard seeds

Heat 2 tbsp of oil in a frying pan and add the mustard seeds. When they pop, add the onions and cook until they turn a golden brown in colour. Add the chopped tomatoes, sambar powder and season with salt and chilli flakes. Add ½ cup of water and bring to the boil. Lower heat and simmer gently until the water has evaporated and a thick sauce is left. Remove from heat.

Serve sprinkled with chopped coriander leaves.

Coconut Sambal

Serves 4

½ cup shredded coconut
1 onion, diced
4 tbsp lemon juice

In a pan, heat 2 tbsp of oil and sauté the onion with salt and chilli flakes to taste. Remove from heat when the onions have browned. Cool the onion mixture and place in a blender with the coconut and 2 tbsp of water, and blend to a paste. If the mixture is too dry add more water 1 tsp at a time. Finally add the lemon juice and blend well.

Serve with dosas.

Potatoes for Dosa Filling
Serves 4

4 potatoes
1 red onion, diced
2 tsp curry powder
2 tbsp lemon juice

Boil the potatoes, and roughly crush with a fork without fully mashing them, and keep aside. Heat 2 tbsp of oil in a frying pan, add the diced onion and fry until browned. Add the curry powder and 2 tbsp water, season with salt and chilli flakes. Stir until the water has evaporated. Add the crushed potatoes and mix together. If the mixture is too dry or sticking to the pan, add 1 tbsp of water then continue to cook whilst stirring. Remove from heat and mix in the lemon juice.

Serve as a filling for the dosas, with coriander as a garnish.

Buttermilk Potatoes
Serves 4

4 potatoes, diced and boiled
1 tsp mustard seeds
1 tsp turmeric powder
1 cup buttermilk

Heat 2 tbsp of oil in a frying pan, then add the mustard seeds and cook until they pop, which should take just a few seconds. Stir in the potatoes and turmeric, then add ½ cup water and bring to the boil. Lower the heat and simmer gently until the water has evaporated and the potatoes are cooked. Add the buttermilk and keep stirring until all the liquid has evaporated.

Serve as a filling for dosas.

Sweet Dosa

Serves 4

1 cup flour
¼ cup rice flour
1 cup jaggery or brown sugar
¼ tsp cardamom powder

In a bowl, add 1½ cups of warm water and dissolve the sugar. In another bowl, add the flour and rice flour with the cardamom powder, stir to mix. Add the sugar mixture to the flour slowly whilst mixing in, ensuring no lumps are formed. Heat a frying pan with a little oil, lower the heat to medium and spoon the mixture into the pan. Spread the mixture using the back of the spoon so that it covers the base in a thin layer. Leave to cook, it will bubble and not have any liquid on the surface when cooked, the underside should be golden brown in colour. Flip it over carefully and cook the other side. When cooked, place onto a plate and fold into quarters.

Serve with fresh fruit and yoghurt.

Sides

Indian Breads

Rice

Raitas

Salads

Chutneys / Pickles

Indian Breads

Bread is an integral part of Indian cuisine and is served with all meals of the day. There are many varieties of Indian breads and some are stuffed with vegetables and some are deep fried, such as the poori. Each region of India has its own specialties. The breads that are most well-known in the UK mostly originate from North India, where the most familiar Indian dishes come from. However, the popular naan bread is an exception. This is a kind of leavened bread with yeast, cooked in a tandoor, thought to have originated from central Asia.

The flat breads are made from whole wheat flour known as 'atta' in Indian. This is mixed with water to form dough and cooked on a 'tava' which is a form of griddle pan. Since many British households do not have a tava, I have chosen to cook the breads in a frying pan in this book. The basic dough for chapatis, on page 127, can be used to make plain chapati or stuffed chapatis.

Rice

Basmati rice is a type of long grain rice and takes its name from the Sanskrit word meaning fragrance, as it is known for its delicate flavour and fragrance. Basmati rice is at the heart of Indian cuisine and has been cultivated at the foot of the Himalayan Mountains in India for thousands of years. As the preferred rice for all Indian dishes, basmati has been used in all the rice dishes included in this book. Bear in mind that when cooked, the rice grains will not stick to each other but will be fluffy in texture.

Raita

Raita is a yoghurt-based accompaniment to a main Indian meal. It has a cooling effect on the palate when eating an overly hot dish, and generally adds flavor and variety to the meal. In my opinion, all Indian meals should have an accompaniment of raita to complement them.

Salads

A salad is a great accompaniment to any Indian meal and a cool refreshing effect on the palate, normally there is a dressing of lemon juice.

Kachumber, recipe on page 158, is a type of Indian salad. "Kacha" in Hindi translates as raw and the salad consists of finely chopped, onions, tomatoes and cucumber with a dressing of lemon juice.

Chutneys / Pickle – Achar

Chutneys are made from fresh fruits and spices. Served with almost every meal, they can be thin or thick in texture and can also be sweet, sour, spicy or mild. Traditional chutney will not have any preservatives added, but are fresh and made with whatever fruits are in season.

Chutneys originated in India and the name comes from the Hindi word 'chatni'. During the colonial era of the British Raj in India, chutney was exported to England and then to other parts of the British empire, such as the Caribbean and South Africa. The British Standard Chutney to be exported was mango chutney called Major Gray chutney. Major Gray was a British army officer based in India during the British occupation reputed to have started the export of chutneys. The Major Gray chutney was first branded by Crosse & Blackwell and is based upon the Indian version. Major Gray chutney is the number one seller in the US, a market in which the Indian version is not sold.

As well as chutneys, this section will also cover pickles or 'achar'. Pickles are produced by drying fruits and vegetables in the sun over a sustained period of time, so no moisture remains and then preserved in oil. The shelf life of these pickles invariably last years. Both chutneys and pickles add brilliant colours and lively flavours to Indian meals.

Chapati / Roti Dough
Makes approx 6

2 cups chapati flour
water

In a bowl, add the chapati flour. Gradually add water and mix with your hands to form a dough, slowly incorporating the flour. The dough should not be too wet but also not too hard either. If too wet, add more flour. Leave the dough to rest for at least an hour before cooking.

Chapati / Roti
Makes approx 6

Chapati dough (see above)
½ cup melted butter

Heat a frying pan. Make small balls with the dough and roll out using a rolling pin into rounds onto a floured work surface. Place into the heated frying pan, and when the underside appears cooked turn over. When the other side is cooked, turn over again. By using a scrunched tea towel, press onto the turned over side of the chapati firmly. The chapatti should puff up. Remove onto a plate. Brush one side with butter. Should the chapati not puff up, don't worry as long as it is cooked through and not doughy.

Serve warm.

Paratha
Makes approx 6

Chapati dough (see page 127)
½ cup melted butter

Heat a frying pan. Make small balls with the dough and roll out with a rolling pin into rounds onto a floured work surface. Brush butter over the rounds. Fold the bottom third into the middle then fold the top third into the middle. Then fold over the sides to form a square shape. Place into the heated frying pan, when the paratha appears cooked on the underside turn over. Brush some butter over the top and turn over again to the other side, and brush some more butter over the other side. Repeat by turning over once more without adding any more butter. There should be small brown spots appearing onto the surface of the paratha when cooked through. Remove onto kitchen paper. Continue until all the dough is used.

Serve.

Lachcha Paratha
Makes approx 6

Chapati dough (see page 127)
½ cup melted butter

Heat a frying pan. Make small balls with the dough and roll out into rounds with a rolling pin onto a floured work surface. Brush butter over the surface of each round and roll into long sausage shapes using your hands. Wrap each long roll into a circle. Press down onto a floured work surface and roll into rounds. Place the rounds into the heated frying pan, when the underside appears cooked, turn over. Brush butter over the cooked side and turn over, brush butter on the other side. Cook until brown spots appear on the surface.

Serve.

Poori

Makes approx 8

Chapati dough (see page 127)
Oil for deep frying

Heat oil in a pan for deep frying. Make small balls with the dough and roll out into small rounds with a rolling pin onto a floured work surface. When the oil is hot, slide the rounds, one at a time, into the frying pan. Using a spatula, press gently onto the rounds and they should puff up. Turn over to cook the other side. Remove onto kitchen paper to drain. Do not worry if they do not puff up.

Serve.

Potato Stuffed Paratha (aloo paratha)
Makes approx 6

Chapati dough (see page 127)
4 tbsp melted butter
1 cup mashed potatoes
1 tsp mango powder

In a bowl, mix the mashed potatoes and mango powder, season with salt and chilli flakes. Heat a frying pan. Make small balls with the dough and roll out with a rolling pin into rounds onto a floured work surface. Add a little of the mashed potato into the middle of the round and bring the ends of the round together to incorporate the mashed potato to form a ball. Press the ball onto a floured work surface. Using a rolling pin roll into a circle, or as close to as possible, ensuring the mashed potato does not escape.

Place the paratha onto the heated frying pan, and when the underside appears cooked turn over. Brush some butter over the top, turn over to the other side and brush some more butter over the other side. Repeat by turning over once more without adding any more butter. There should be small brown spots appearing onto the surface of the paratha when cooked through. Remove onto kitchen paper. Continue until all the dough and mashed potatoes are used.

Serve warm with plain yoghurt and / or chutney.

Sweet Paratha
Makes approx 6

Chapati dough (see page 127)
4 tbsp melted butter
½ cup sugar

Heat a frying pan. Make small balls with the dough and roll out with a rolling pin into rounds onto a floured work surface. Brush butter over the rounds and sprinkle approx 1 tbsp of sugar onto the rounds. Fold the bottom third into the middle then fold the top third into the middle. Then fold over the sides to form a square shape. Place into the heated frying pan, and when the underside appears cooked turn over. Brush some butter over the top, turn over to the other side and brush some more butter over the other side. Repeat by turning over once more without adding any more butter. There should be small brown spots appearing onto the surface of the paratha when cooked through. Remove onto kitchen paper. Continue until all the dough is used up.

Serve warm with plain yoghurt and / or chutney.

Mango Paratha
Serves 4

Chapati dough (see page 127)
2 tbsp spicy mango chutney

Heat a frying pan. Make small balls with the dough and roll out with a rolling pin into rounds onto a floured work surface. Spread mango chutney over the rounds. Fold the bottom third into the middle then fold the top third into the middle. Then fold over the sides to form a square shape. Place into the heated frying pan, and when the underside appears cooked turn over. Brush some butter over the top, turn over to the other side and brush some more butter over the other side. Repeat by turning over once more without adding more butter. There should be small brown spots appearing onto the surface of the paratha when cooked through. Remove onto kitchen paper. Continue until all the dough is used up.

Serve warm with plain yoghurt and / or chutney.

Mint Paratha
Makes approx 6

2 cups chapati flour
4 tbsp melted butter
½ cup fresh mint leaves, washed and finely chopped
2 tsp mango powder

In a bowl, mix the flour with the mint leaves and mango powder, season with salt and chilli flakes. Using your hands gradually add water and form a dough, slowly incorporating the flour. The dough should not be too wet, but not too hard either. If too wet, add more flour. Leave the dough to rest for at least an hour.

Heat a frying pan. Make small balls with the dough and roll out with a rolling pin into rounds onto a floured work surface. Place onto the heated frying pan, and when the underside appears cooked turn over. Brush some butter over the top, turn over to the other side and brush some more butter over the other side. Repeat by turning over once more, without adding oil. There should be small brown spots appearing on the surface of the paratha when cooked through. Remove onto a plate. Continue until all the dough is used up.

Serve.

Cumin and Chilli Chapati
Makes approx 6

2 cups chapati flour
1 tbsp cumin seeds

In a frying pan add the cumin seeds and dry roated until they change colour and release their aroma. Remove into a pestle and mortar and crush to a powder. In a bowl, mix the flour with the crushed cumin seeds, season with salt and chilli flakes. Using your hands gradually add water and form a dough, slowly incorporating the flour. The dough should not be too wet, but not too hard either. If too wet, add more flour. Leave the dough to rest for at least an hour. Heat oil in a pan for deep frying. Make small balls with the dough and roll out into rounds with a rolling pin onto a floured work surface. When the oil is hot, slide the rounds into the frying pan. Using a spatula, press gently onto the rounds and they should puff up (don't worry if they don't). Turn over to cook the other side. Remove onto kitchen paper. Continue until all the dough is used up.

Serve.

Mint and Kalonji Seed Paratha
Serves 4

2 cups chapati flour
¼ cup mint leaves, finely chopped
2 tsp black onion seeds / kalonji seeds
½ cup plain yoghurt

In a bowl, mix the flour with the mint leaves and kalonji seeds, season with salt and chilli flakes. Add the yoghurt and incorporate into the mixture. Using your hands gradually add water and form a dough. The dough should not be too wet but not too hard either. If too wet, add more flour. Leave the dough to rest for at least an hour.

Heat a frying pan. Make small balls with the dough and roll out with a rolling pin into rounds onto a floured work surface. Place onto the heated frying pan, and when the underside appears cooked turn over. Brush some butter over the top, turn over to the other side and brush some more butter over the turned over side. Repeat by turning over once more, without adding more water. There should be small brown spots appearing on the surface of the paratha when cooked through. Remove onto a plate. Continue until all the dough is used.

Serve.

Naan
Makes approx 6

500g plain flour
7g sachet dried yeast
1 tsp sugar
¼ cup plain yoghurt

In small bowl, stir the yeast and sugar with a little warm water, then leave to stand for 10 minutes to ferment. In another bowl, add the flour and make a well in the middle. Pour the fermented yeast mixture into the centre of the flour. Add the yoghurt and using your hands make dough, adding extra warm water if needed. The dough should not be sticky, but firm and not too dry. Cover with a tea towel and let it rise for about 2 hours until it doubles in size. Knead the dough on a floured work surface for about 5 minutes. Make small balls of the dough and roll flat. Place the flattened dough onto a greased baking tray and lightly spread a little butter or oil over the top, then bake in the oven for 15 minutes at 180°C or until browned. Spread more melted butter over the top before serving.

Serve warm.

Peshwari Naan
Makes approx 6

Naan dough (see page 137)
½ cup raisins
½ cup desiccated coconut
½ cup flaked almonds

In a bowl, mix the raisins, coconut and almond flakes and keep aside. Divide the naan dough mixture into approximately 6 pieces and roll each one out flat onto a floured work surface. Place equal amounts of the fruit mixture into each of the naans and fold the sides in to secure the fruit mixture. Roll the naans out flat again. Place the naans onto a greased baking tray and spread a little melted butter over the top. Place in a preheated oven at 180°C and bake for 15 minutes, or until browned.

Serve warm with more melted butter over the top.

Missi Roti
Makes approx 6

1 cup chapati flour
1 cup besan (chickpea flour)
2 tbsp dried fenugreek leaves / kasoori methi
1 tsp toasted cumin seeds

Place all the ingredients into a bowl, season with salt and chilli flakes. Using your hands, gradually add water to form a dough. The dough should not be sticky, but firm. Cover with a tea towel and leave for 1 hour. Make small balls of the dough and roll flat onto a floured work surface. Heat a frying pan and lower the heat to medium, place the round roti onto it. Cook until brown spots appear on the underside. When one side is done, about 1-2 minutes, turn over. Brush some oil over the top, and turn over again and brush oil over the other side and turn over to cook again. Remove and place onto a plate and spread with butter before serving. Continue until all the dough is used.

Serve with chutney and/or butter.

Bhatura / fluffy fried Bread
Makes approx 6

2 cups self-rising flour
½ tsp baking powder
½ cup plain yoghurt
1 tsp sugar

Place all the ingredients into a bowl. Using your hands add water gradually, mixing into a soft dough. Cover with a damp cloth and leave for 1 hour. Knead the dough on a floured work surface, then divide into small balls and roll these out on a floured work surface, into rounds. Heat some oil in a pan for deep frying, when the oil is hot slide the round bhutra into the pan of oil. When frying, press lightly onto the bhutra with a spatula, which should make them rise, then turn over and cook the other side. Remove onto kitchen paper. Continue until all the dough is used.

Serve with chickpea curry / channa masala (see page 108).

Garlic and Coriander Naan
Serves 4

4 plain naan breads
½ tsp garlic paste
4 tbsp melted butter
1 tbsp fresh coriander chopped finely

Pre heat the oven at 180°C. In a bowl, mix melted butter with the garlic paste and the chopped coriander. Place the naan breads onto a greased baking tray and spread mixture over the top. Place in the oven and bake for 15 minutes or until browned.

Serve warm.

Mango Naan Bread
Serves 4

2 plain naan breads
2 tbsp mango chutney

Warm the naan bread under the grill for about 1 minute on each side. Spread mango chutney thinly over the top. Cut the naan bread into quarters.

Serve.

Easy Chilli Coriander Naan Bread
Serves 2

2 naan breads
1 tsp chilli flakes
1 tsp chopped fresh coriander leaves
 2 tsp melted butter

Place the naan bread under a grill to warm. Remove the naan bread, and brush with melted butter. Sprinkle with salt, chilli flakes and coriander leaves over the top. Return to the grill to heat for another minute. Remove onto a plate.

Serve.

Garlic and Coriander Bread
Serves 2

1 plain baguette
1 tbsp garlic paste
2 tsp coriander paste
2 tbsp melted butter

In a small bowl, mix the melted butter with the garlic paste and coriander and keep aside. Make deep diagonal slashes in the baguette without cutting all the way through. Carefully spoon the mixture into the slashes of the baguette. Bake in the oven for 20 minutes at 180°C.

Serve warm.

Coriander Toast
Serves 4

1 small loaf of bread, cut into thick slices
1 cup chopped coriander leaves (or coriander paste if leaves unavailable)
4 tbsp oil

In a bowl, add the oil and mix with the coriander, then keep aside. Toast one side of the bread slices under a grill, turn over and brush the untoasted sides with the coriander mixture. Place onto a baking tray with the untoasted sides up and bake in the oven for 5 minutes at 180°C.

Serve.

Makki di Roti
Makes approx 6

1 cup maize flour
½ tsp salt or to taste
butter for spreading

In a bowl mix the maize flour with salt, make a well in the middle of the flour, make a dough using your hands by adding warm water. The dough should be soft but not sticky. Heat a small frying pan until hot, turn the heat down to medium. Make small balls of the dough and roll each ball of dough on a floured work surface, into a round. Place the roti onto the frying pan and cook for about 30 seconds, turn over and brush a little butter onto the top side, turn over and brush butter over the other side. Cook the roti turning over once more without adding more butter. When cooked, it should have small brown spots and turn a golden brown colour. Remove from heat and spread some more butter over the top before serving. Continue until all the dough is used.

Serve with Saag.

Rice

Plain Basmati Rice
Serves 4

1 cup basmati rice

Wash the rice in several changes of water. Place into a saucepan with a lid, and add just under 2 cups of water and stir. Add 1 tsp salt if desired. Bring to boil, then lower the heat and cover with the lid. Simmer for 15 to 20 minutes until the rice is cooked and the water has evaporated. When cooked, leave the lid on until serving. Fluff the rice with a fork when serving.

Serve.

Yellow Rice
Serves 4

1 cup basmati rice
½ tsp turmeric powder

Wash the rice in several changes of water. Place into a saucepan with a lid; add turmeric and season with salt to taste. Add just under 2 cups of water and stir. Bring to boil and lower heat. Cover the pan with the lid and simmer for 15 minutes until the rice is cooked and the water has evaporated. When cooked, leave the lid on until serving. Fluff the rice with a fork when serving.

Serve.

Cumin Rice
Serves 2

1 cup basmati rice
1 tsp cumin seeds

Wash rice in several changes of water and keep aside. In a lidded pan, heat 1 tbsp oil, add the cumin seeds and cook until they change colour. Add the rice with just under 2 cups of water to the pan, season with salt and chilli flakes, stir and bring to the boil. Lower the heat and place the lid on the pan simmer for 15 minutes until the rice is cooked and all the water has been absorbed. Keep an eye on the rice to ensure it does not burn. When cooked, leave the lid on until serving. Fluff the rice with a fork when serving.

Serve.

Lentils and Rice
Serves 4

1 onion, chopped finely
1 cup bastmati rice
½ cup red lentils
2 tbsp korma paste

Wash the lentils and rice in several changes of water and keep aside. In a saucepan with a lid, heat 2 tbsp oil, add the chopped onion and cook until they turn a golden brown colour. Add the lentils and rice and stir for 1 minute. Stir in the curry paste and continue cooking for a further minute. Add 2 cups of water and bring to the boil. Lower the heat, and cover with a lid and simmer gently until the rice and lentils are cooked, about 20 minutes. Keep an eye on the pan so that it does not boil over or burn. When cooked, leave the lid on until serving. Fluff the rice with a fork when serving.

Serve.

Kitchri
Serves 4

1 cup basmati rice
1 cup red lentils
1 tsp cumin seeds
1 tsp garam masala

Wash the rice and lentils in several changes of water and keep aside. Heat 2 tbsp oil in a saucepan with a lid, add the cumin seeds and fry until they turn a darker brown colour. Add the rice, lentils and garam masala, season with salt and stir. Add 3 cups of water and bring to the boil. Lower the heat and cover with a lid, simmer for 20 minutes until the rice and lentils are cooked and tender. When cooked, leave the lid on until serving. Fluff the rice with a fork when serving.

Serve.
Optional: Serve with chopped coriander mixed into the kitchri.

Sunshine Coconut Rice
Serves 4

2 cups basmati rice
400ml coconut cream
½ tsp turmeric powder

Wash the rice in several changes of water. In a saucepan with a lid, stir together the washed rice, turmeric, coconut cream and 2 cups of water. Bring to the boil, then lower heat and cover with a lid, simmer until the rice is cooked, about 15 minutes. Keep checking the rice to ensure it does not burn. When cooked, leave the lid on until serving. Fluff the rice with a fork when serving.

Serve.

Rice Salad
Serves 4

2 cups cold cooked yellow rice (see page 144)
1 red pepper, chopped finely
½ red onion, chopped finely
2 tbsp vinaigrette dressing

In a bowl, mix all the ingredients together.

Raita

To make the yoghurt thinner, add some milk whilst mixing to obtain the right consistency for your raita.

Raita
Serves 4

1 cup plain yoghurt
¼ tsp cumin powder
¼ tsp garam masala

In a bowl, beat the yoghurt with a little salt, chilli flakes, cumin and garam masala, stirring to mix.

Serve.

Mint Raita
Serves 4

1 cup plain yoghurt
2-3 tsp mint sauce, or to taste
½ tsp cumin powder

In a bowl, beat the yoghurt, mint sauce, cumin powder, season with salt and chilli flakes.

Serve cold.

Cucumber Raita
Serves 4

1 cup plain yoghurt
2 inch piece of cucumber, chopped into small pieces
¼ tsp cumin powder

In a bowl beat the yoghurt, chopped cucumber and ground cumin powder with a little salt and chilli flakes.

Serve.

Onion and Tomato Raita
Serves 4

1 cup plain yoghurt
½ red onion, finely chopped
1 tomato, finely diced
1 tsp cumin seeds

In a frying pan, dry roast the cumin seeds. Remove and crush in a pestle and mortar, and keep aside. In another bowl beat the yoghurt and mix in the crushed cumin seeds, along with the chopped onion and tomato, season with salt and chilli flakes.

Serve.

Pomegranate Raita
Serves 4

1 cup plain yoghurt
2 tbsp pomegranate seeds
¼ tsp cumin powder
¼ tsp chaat masala

In a bowl, beat the yoghurt and cumin powder. Mix in the pomegranate seeds, and season with salt. Sprinkle with chilli flakes and chaat masala before serving.

Serve.

Boondi Raita
Serves 4

1 cup plain yoghurt
¼ cup boondi (small savoury balls; available from Indian stores)
½ tsp ground cumin powder

In a bowl, beat the yoghurt and keep aside. In another bowl, add the boondi and cover with warm water. When they have soaked for about 5 minutes but no longer, carefully squeeze the liquid out of them. Make sure that they are not mashed, but still retain their round ball shapes. Add these to the yoghurt, stir in cumin powder and season with salt and chilli flakes.

Serve.

Melon and Cucumber Raita

Serves 4

½ cucumber, diced into small cubes
¼ melon, diced into small cubes
2 cups plain yoghurt
Handful of fresh mint leaves

In a bowl, mix together all the ingredients along with a little salt and chilli flakes, to taste.

Serve.

Pineapple Raita

Serves 4

1 cup plain yoghurt
2 slices of pineapple cubed
1 tsp cumin ground
Handful of pomegranate seeds

Mix yoghurt and cumin powder, season with salt and chilli flakes. Stir in the cubed pineapple and a handful of pomegranate seeds.

Serve.

Carrot and Onion Raita

Serves 4

1 carrot, grated
1 small red onion, finely chopped
1 tbsp fresh mint leaves, finely chopped
1 cup plain yoghurt

Mix all the ingredients together and season with salt and chilli flakes.

Serve.

Optional: Add ½ tsp ground cumin powder.

Carrot and Date Raita

Serves 4

2 carrots, grated
1 tsp black mustard seeds
2 cups plain yoghurt
½ cup dates, pitted and chopped (roughly 12 dates)

In a bowl, mix together the grated carrots, chopped dates and plain yoghurt, and keep aside. In a frying pan, heat 1 tbsp of oil, add the mustard seeds and cook until they pop, this should be almost immediate. Pour the mustard seeds into the yoghurt mixture and season with salt and chilli flakes, stir to combine.

Serve.

Indian Salad
Serves 4

½ cucumber, finely sliced
2 tomatoes, diced
½ iceberg lettuce, chopped
½ red onion, sliced into rings

In a bowl, mix all the ingredients together.

Serve sprinkled with fresh chopped coriander leaves or fresh chopped mint leaves as garnish.

Yoghurt Dressing
Serves 4

1 cup plain yoghurt
1 tbsp lime juice
1 tbsp of mint sauce

Mix together yoghurt, mint sauce and lime juice, season with salt and chilli flakes to taste.

Use as a dressing for salads.

Melon Ball Salad

Serves 4

750g mixed melons, cut into balls using melon baller
¼ cup fresh mint leaves
½ cup orange juice

In a bowl, mix all the ingredients together.

Serve.

Indian Salad Dressing

Serves 4

½ cup fresh lime juice
5cm ginger, sliced into thin strips
¼ cup fresh chopped coriander
1 fresh green chilli, finely chopped

In a bowl, mix all the ingredients together.

Serve over a green salad.

Tomato, Mint and Lime Salad

Serves 4

4 tomatoes, chopped into wedges
4 green shallots, chopped
½ cup chopped fresh mint leaves
¼ cup lime juice

In a bowl, mix all the ingredients together and season with salt and chilli flakes.

Serve.

Pineapple and Cucumber Salad

Serves 4

450g tin of diced pineapple (in its own juice)
1 small cucumber, diced
1 fresh red chilli, diced
¼ cup lime juice

In a bowl, mix all the ingredients together.

Serve with sprinkled coriander as garnish, as an accompaniment to any meat dish.

Chickpea and Tomato Salad
Serves 4

400g tinned chickpeas
1 potato peeled, boiled and cut into cubes
2 tsp chaat masala
2 tomatoes, chopped finely

Place the chickpeas in a colander and wash thoroughly, keep aside. In a frying pan, heat 2 tbsp oil, add the potatoes and chickpeas, season with salt and chilli flakes, and add ¼ cup water and bring to boil. Lower heat and simmer until the potatoes and chickpeas are cooked and tender. Remove into a bowl and allow to cool. When cold, mix in the tomatoes and chaat masala.

Serve sprinkled with chopped coriander as a garnish.

Chilli and Onion Salad
Serves 2

1 small red onion, finely diced
2 small green chillies, finely chopped
½ cup lemon juice

In a bowl, mix the diced onions with the chopped chillies. Add lemon juice, salt and chilli flakes to taste. Toss together until thoroughly mixed.

Serve.
Optional: Can use white wine vinegar instead of lemon juice.

Onion and Tomato Salad
Serves 2

1 red onion, sliced into rounds
2 tomatoes, sliced into rounds
Handful of chopped fresh coriander leaves
½ cup of lemon juice

On a plate, arrange the slices of red onion and tomato, season with some salt and chilli flakes. Sprinkle the coriander leaves as garnish and drizzle with lemon juice.

Serve.

Pomegranate Salad
Serves 2

2 tbsp pomegranate seeds
½ red onion, diced
1 tbsp lemon juice
½ cucumber, diced

Mix all the ingredients together and season with salt and chilli flakes to taste.

Serve.

Spicy Cottage Cheese Spread

Serves 2

1 300g tub cottage cheese
1 tsp salt, to taste
1½ tsp black pepper or chilli flakes, to taste

In a bowl, mix cottage cheese with salt and chilli flakes or black pepper to taste.

Serve with a jacket potato.

Spicy Coleslaw

Serves 2

1 300g tub of coleslaw
1 tsp salt, to taste
1 ½ tsp black pepper or chilli flakes, to taste

In a bowl, mix coleslaw with salt and chilli flakes or black pepper to taste.

Serve with a jacket potato.

Mango Salsa
Serves 2

1 mango, skinned and diced
½ tsp black mustard seeds
1 tsp sugar
2 curry leaves

Place the diced mango in a saucepan with 1 cup of water and 1 tsp of sugar and a pinch of salt. Stirring continually bring the mixture to the boil. Cook for about 10 minutes until no liquid is left in the pan. In another frying pan, heat 1 tbsp of oil, add the curry leaves, chilli flakes and mustard seeds, when the seeds pop, remove from heat. Pour over the mango.

Serve.

Kachumber
Serves 4

1 red onion, finely chopped
2 tomatoes, finely chopped
2 tbsp lemon juice
½ large cucumber, finely diced

In bowl, mix together the onions, tomatoes and cucumber. Add the lemon juice and season with salt and chilli flakes. Taste and add more lemon juice if required.

Serve sprinkled with coriander leaves as garnish.

Tamarind Chutney (imli)
Serves 4

1 tbsp tamarind paste
1 tsp cumin powder
2 tsp brown sugar

Mix together the tamarind paste, cumin powder and brown sugar in a bowl, season with salt and chilli flakes to taste. Gradually add ½ cup warm water whilst stirring to prevent lumps forming, obtaining an almost batter-like consistency which is not too runny and not too thick. Leave aside for about an hour to thicken slightly. Taste, and if too tart, add more sugar, if the consistency is too thick add more warm water.

Serve as a dip or an accompaniment.

Ginger Pickle
Serves 4

50g fresh ginger, cut into small pieces
2 tsp tamarind paste
½ tsp sugar

In a pan, heat 2 tbsp of oil and sauté the ginger for about 2 mins. Add salt and chilli flakes and cook for a further 1 minute. Remove from heat and add 2 tsp tamarind paste and the sugar along with ¼ cup water. Return to the heat and bring to the boil, lower the heat and simmer until the all the liquid has evaporated. Store in an airtight container.

Serve.

Coriander / Green Chutney
Serves 4

1 bunch of fresh coriander leaves
1 onion, finely chopped
1 tsp cumin powder
2 tsp mango powder

Place all the ingredients into a blender with ¼ cup water, season with salt and chilli flakes. Blend finely, adding more water if required.

Serve.

Tamarind and Date Chutney
Serves 2

1 cup tamarind chutney (see page 159)
½ cup dates pitted and chopped (about 12 dates)

Heat 1 cup of water in a small saucepan, add the dates and bring mixture to the boil for about 20 minutes or until the dates are soft. Remove from heat and cool. Add the dates to the tamarind chutney and stir to combine.

Serve.

Chilli and Onion Chutney
Serves 4

1 onion, chopped
2 tsp chilli powder
1 tbsp tamarind paste
1 tsp mustard seeds

In a blender, add the onions, chilli powder and tamarind paste, adding salt to taste and ¼ cup of water. Blend to a smooth paste and keep aside. In a frying pan, heat 4 tbsp of oil and drop in the mustard seeds, when they pop, almost immediately, add the blended onions and cook stirring all the time. When the mixture comes together and the oil separates from the mixture in the pan, remove from heat.

Serve as a spread or accompaniment.

Apple and Mint Chutney
Serves 4

2 cooking apples, peeled and chopped
4 tbsp lemon juice
4 tbsp fresh mint leaves

Place all the ingredients in a blender with ¼ cup water, season with salt and chilli flakes. Blend finely, adding more water if required. Taste and add more lemon juice if required.

Serve.

Chilli Coconut Chutney
Serves 4

1 cup shredded coconut
2 tsp chilli powder
2 tsp cumin seeds

Heat a frying pan and when hot add the cumin seeds, and dry roast until they change colour. Remove from pan and place into a blender with the coconut, chilli powder and season with salt. Add ½ cup of water and blend, the mixture should have a smooth consistency. Add more water if required to get the right consistency.

Serve.

Coriander and Lime Chutney
Serves 4

½ small jar spicy mango chutney
4 tbsp lime juice
½ small onion, finely diced
1 bunch of fresh coriander, finely chopped

Place all the ingredients together into a blender, season with salt. Add chilli flakes if the mango chutney is not very spicy. Blend together until smooth.

Serve with poppadoms.

Mint Chutney
Serves 4

1 bunch of fresh mint leaves
1 onion, chopped
2 tsp pomegranate powder

Place all the ingredients into a blender, add ¼ cup of water, and season with salt and chilli flakes. Blend until smooth, adding more water if required.

Serve.

Pineapple Chutney
Serves 2

400g tinned pineapple cubes (in their own juice)
2 tbsp sugar
1 tsp black mustard seeds
1 tsp onion seeds

In a saucepan, add the tinned pineapple pieces and their juice with the sugar. Bring to the boil. Lower the heat and simmer until the pineapple has broken down and is soft. There should be very little water left. Remove from the heat and keep aside. In a frying pan, heat 1 tbsp of oil, add the mustard and onion seeds and cook until they pop. Add the cooked pineapple to the pan, season with salt and chilli flakes, stir to combine and cook for a further 1 minute ensuring all the liquid has evaporated. Remove and cool before serving.

Serve.

Mango Chilli Chutney

Serves 4

1 mango, skinned and diced finely
1 red onion, finely chopped
2 tbsp sweet chilli sauce
2 tbsp lime juice

In bowl mix all the ingredients together, seasoning with a little salt.

Serve.
Optional: Place 1 tbsp of the chutney onto lettuce leaves.

Cranberry Chutney

Serves 4

1 cup cranberries
1 tsp cumin seeds
2 tbsp brown sugar
Handful of fresh coriander leaves

Heat 2 tbsp oil in a frying pan, add the cumin seeds and cook until they change colour. Add the cranberries, seasoning with salt and chilli flakes. Add ½ cup water and bring the mixture to the boil, lower heat and simmer until the cranberries have softened, about 15 - 20 minutes. Add the brown sugar and coriander leaves, and mix. When the sugar has dissolved, remove from the heat and allow to cool. Pour the mixture into a blender and blend until smooth. Pour into a bowl, and cool before serving.

Serve
Optional: Use fresh green chillies instead of chilli flakes. Thin slices of ginger can be cooked and then blended with the cranberries.

Indian Sweets

Indian cuisine is famous throughout the world for its sweets, which are called 'mithai' in Indian. Sweets play an important role in Indian culture. Every special occasion or event is marked with the giving of sweets, such as at Diwali, weddings, parties, and even when visiting friends and relatives. To add to their appeal, sweets can sometimes have a very thin wrapping of silver paper on them called 'varakh.'

Indian sweets are either milk-based, such as burfi, or flour-based, such as halva. The most famous Indian sweets also often find their way onto Indian grocery shops and onto restaurants menus in the UK. Rasgulla is known to be the most popular sweet in India, and is made of small sweet balls which can be in a variety of colours and are coated in a sugar syrup. Khoa is a milk-based sweet which can then be made into other sweets by adding nuts or fruits such as almonds and or raisins. Kulfi is a popular dessert and is known as the Indian version of ice cream. Kheer is another popular dessert in Indian households and essentially it is rice pudding, but can have nuts or dried fruits added, such as almonds or raisins.

Rosewater is often used in sweets and desserts for added flavour.

Almond Kulfi
Serves 4/6

400ml evaporated milk
300g sweet condensed milk
300ml whipping cream
1 tbsp ground almonds

Place evaporated milk, condensed milk and cream into a saucepan. Bring to the boil, stirring continually. Lower the heat and simmer gently until the mixture has reduced by half. Remove from the heat and allow to cool. When cool, add the ground almonds and stir to combine. Pour into kulfi moulds or small ramekins, and place in freezer until hardened. To serve, remove from freezer and stand in hot water to ease the kulfi out of the pot, but not for too long as you don't want the kulfi to melt.

Serve.
Optional: Sprinkle with pistachio nuts.

Cardamom Ice Cream
Serves 4/6

225ml sweetened condensed milk
600ml light evaporated milk
1 tsp cardamom powder or crushed cardamom pods

In a blender, blend all the ingredients together. Pour mixture into a container and place in freezer. When frozen remove from freezer and blend again until smooth. Repeat the blend and freeze once more.

Alternatively churn in an ice cream maker.

Serve.
Optional: Sprinkle with chopped mixed nuts.

Rose Rice Pudding
Serves 4/6

4 tbsp of basmati rice
4 tbsp sugar
2 tsp rose water
1 litre of milk

Wash rice in several changes of water and place in a saucepan with a lid. Add the milk and bring to the boil, stirring all the time. Lower the heat, and cover the pan with a lid and simmer until the milk has reduced and the rice is cooked. Keep an eye on the pan as the milk may bubble to the top and spill over. When the rice is cooked, add the sugar and rose water and stir to dissolve the sugar. When cooked, remove from stove pour into glass serving bowls.

Serve hot or cold.
Optional: Sprinkle with chopped mixed nuts.

Sweet Balls (peda)
Serves 2

1 cup milk powder, plus extra for making 1 cup milk
1 cup homemade paneer, crumbled (see page 80)
¾ cup icing sugar
3 tbsp melted butter

Make 1 cup of milk using milk powder and water, as per packet instructions, and keep aside. In a deep wok-style pan, heat the melted butter and add the crumbled paneer, milk powder and the reserved milk. Whilst stirring on a medium heat, cook for at least 10 minutes. The mixture will come together and form an almost dough-like consistency. Take off the heat and place into a bowl. When the mixture is cool to handle, mix in the sugar with your hands into the dough. Once the sugar has been incorporated into the mixture, break small sections of the dough and roll in to balls in the plam of your hands. Place the balls onto a plate and using your thumb, make an indent on the top of each.

Serve.
Optional: Place slivered almonds, pistachios or ground cardamom into the indents on the peda.

Carrot Halva
Serves 4/6

5 carrots, grated
1 litre milk
6 tbsp of sugar
2 tbsp butter

In a saucepan, add the grated carrots and the milk. Bring to the boil whilst stirring. Lower the heat and simmer, stirring frequently, ensure the mixture does not boil over or stick to the bottom of the pan. When the milk has been completely asorbed and no liquid remains, add the sugar and butter and keep stirring for a further 5 minutes, to ensure all liquid produced by the addition of the sugar has been absorbed. Continue stirring and cook for a further 5 minutes. Remove into a glass dish and spread evenly. Allow to cool completely and cut into squares.

Serve.
Optional: Can be served with ice cream. Also, crushed green cardamom seeds can be added with the sugar and butter.

Sweet Vermicelli
Serves 4/6

1 cup vermicelli
5 cups milk
½ cup sugar
½ tbsp butter

Heat butter in a small saucepan and fry the vermicelli until golden brown in colour. Add the milk and bring to the boil, lower the heat and cook for about 20 minutes until the mixture thickens. Add sugar and stir to dissolve. Pour into glass bowls or dessert glasses and serve hot.

Optional: Add ½ tbsp rosewater at the same time as the sugar for an exotic flavour.

Coconut Ice Cream Balls
Serves 2

8 vanilla ice cream scoops
6 tbsp shredded coconut

Place shredded coconut onto a plate and roll the scooped ice cream into the coconut, and form 8 balls.

Serve in a small bowl, with a sprig of mint.

Almond Burfi
Serves 4

200g ground almonds
200g sugar
150ml single cream
75g butter

In a saucepan, melt the butter. Add the ground almonds, sugar and cream. Keep stirring on a low heat for about 15 minutes, ensuring the mixture does not stick. When the mixture turns a darker colour, remove from the heat and pour into a dish. Sprinkle some chopped almonds over the top. Let it cool and then cut into squares.

Serve.

Semolina Squares
Serves 4

½ cup sugar
½ cup milk
125g butter
½ cup fine semolina

In a saucepan, heat the milk, sugar and 1 cup water. Bring to the boil and stir until the sugar has dissolved. In another saucepan melt the butter, add the semolina and stir until the semolina turns a golden brown colour. Add the milk and sugar mixture to the semolina, be careful as the mixture may splatter and bubble, lower the heat and simmer whilst stirring until mixture has thickened, which should take about 5 minutes. Spread mixture into a greased shallow cake tin, and cool then place in the fridge until firm. When cold, take out the fridge and cut into squares.

Serve
Optional: Combine ½ tsp cinnamon and 2 tbsp sugar together and sprinkle onto squares before placing in the fridge to cool.

Fruit Salad
Serves 4/6

500g of mixed fruit such as apples, pears, bananas, pineapple, cut into small cubes,
2 tsp chaat masala

Place the cubes of fruit into a bowl and sprinkle chaat masala over the fruit and toss to combine.

Serve in small bowls.

Tapioca Kheer / Pudding
Serves 4

½ cup tapioca pearls
⅓ cup sugar or to taste
4 green cardamom pods, broken
500ml milk

In a bowl, soak the tapioca pearl seeds for about 20 minutes. In a saucepan, heat the milk with the cardamom pods and sugar, stir to dissolve the sugar. When the sugar has dissolved, add the drained tapioca pearls and ½ cup water. Bring to the boil, then lower the heat and simmer gently, stirring occasionally until the tapioca pearls become translucent. Remove from heat and serve into bowls, taking out the cardamom pods.

Serve.

Ricotta Rasamali
Serves 4/6

500g ricotta cheese
¼ cup sugar
2 cups single cream
1 tsp green cardamom seeds ground

Place a muslin cloth over a colander and pour in the ricotta cheese. Tie the muslin cloth and squeeze and drain as much liquid as possible from the cheese. Drain for about an hour. Once drained, mix the cheese, sugar and ½ tsp green cardamom seeds together and spread into a one litre baking tray. Bake at 180°C for 40 to 45 minutes, ensuring that it keeps its colour. Remove from oven and cool at room temperature and cut into 2 cm squares.

Place the squares into a deep bowl and keep aside. In a saucepan, add the cream with ½ tsp of ground cardamom seeds, heat stirring all the time, until the cream has reduced and thickened. Pour over the top of the rasmali squares, and place in the fridge to chill.

Serve cold in small bowls.
Optional: Decorate with pistachio nuts when serving.

Doughnuts
Makes 25/30

2 ¼ cups self-rising flour
½ cup ground almonds
⅓ cup plain yoghurt
100g melted butter

In a bowl, mix the self-rising flour and ground almonds. Rub in butter until the mixture resembles breadcrumbs. Add the yoghurt and using your hands form a dough of the mixture. On a floured work surface, knead the dough until smooth. Divide the dough into small balls and flatten just a little. Heat oil in a deep pan and deep fry the doughnuts for about 5 minutes until golden brown in colour. Don't overcrowd the frying pan as the balls will expand a little and keep turning them to get an even colour. Drain on absorbent paper.

Serve. Roll the balls in sugar, before serving with sweet yoghurt.
Optional: Add 1 tsp of rose water for an exotic flavor or soak in sugar syrup.

Sweet Yoghurt

1 cup plain yoghurt
1 tbsp icing sugar
1 tsp rose water

Mix together yoghurt, icing sugar and rose water.

Serve with the doughnuts.
Tip: Add a little milk to thin the yoghurt to obtain the right consistency.

Fruit Custard
Serves 4/6

420g tinned mixed fruit
150g carton ready made custard

In a sauce pan, heat the custard until hot and pour into a serving jug. Spoon some fruit into individual bowls and pour the custard over the top of the fruit.

Serve.

Pineapple with Chilli and Lime Syrup
Serves 4/6

1 pineapple, cut into thin slices
½ cup sugar
2 red chillies
1 lime rind and juice

In a saucepan, heat the sugar and 100 ml of water, stir until the sugar has dissolved. Add the chillies and bring to the boil. Continue to boil until the mixture takes on a syrupy consistency. Allow to cool. When cooled add the lime rind and juice into the syrup. On a serving plate, lay out the pineapple slices and drizzle the syrup over the pineapple. Place in the fridge to chill.

Serve chilled with ice cream.

Microwave Milk Burfi
Serves 4/6

2 cups milk powder
300ml double cream
400ml condensed milk
1 tsp cardamom powder

Mix all the ingredients together until you achieve a smooth consistency, then pour into a deep rectangle or square microwave bowl. Place the bowl in the microwave and cook for 5 minutes. Keep an eye on the bowl and if it appears to boil over, stop the microwave and let the mixture cool, then start the microwave again. After 5 minutes, take the dish out and stir well. Place the bowl back into the microwave and cook for a further 5 minutes. Take the dish out of the microwave and stir again. Repeat process once more. After the third time, take out and cool, when cold cut into squares, using a sharp knife.

Serve as a treat.

Yellow Sweet Rice

Serves 4/6

1 cup basmati rice
½ cup sugar
½ tsp yellow food colouring
¼ cup slivered almonds

Wash the rice in several changes of water and keep aside. In a saucepan with a lid, heat about 1 tbsp oil and add the slivered almonds, stirring all the time, cook the almonds until the almonds have browned. Add the washed rice with 2 cups of water, to the pan and stir in the yellow food colour. Bring to the boil, then lower the heat and simmer with the lid on the saucepan until the rice is cooked and tender and all the water has evaporated. When cooked, fluff the rice with a fork before serving.

Serve hot or cold.
Optional: A few strands of saffron can be added, along with almonds.

Mango Custard

Serves 4

150g carton ready made custard
1 ripe mango, pureed (or use a tin of pureed mango)
1 tsp lime juice
½ cup milk

Place the mango puree into a saucepan and heat until warm but not boiling. Add the lime juice and stir for about 1 to 2 minutes. Add the custard to the pan and the milk. Stir until boiling and the mixture thickens slightly, ensuring the mixture does not stick to the bottom of the pan. Pour into glass bowls or dessert glasses and place in the fridge to cool.

Serve cold, decorated with slices of mango.

Cinnamon Peaches

Serves 4

4 firm peaches
20 cloves
½ cup cinnamon sugar

Gently peel away the skin of the peaches using a paring knife. Stick 5 cloves into each peach. Sprinkle the cinnamon sugar on a plate, reserving 4 tsp of the sugar, and roll the peaches in the sugar on the plate and place onto separate sheets of foil, for each peach. Sprinkle 1 tsp sugar over the top of each peach, close the foil around each of the peaches. Grill on a barbecue or bake in the oven for 25 minutes at 180°C, until the peaches are warm and soft. When serving, open each peach parcel onto a plate to avoid losing the peach juice.

Serve hot with ice cream.

Gulab Jamun
Serves 4/6

1 cup milk powder, plus extra to make milk for dough
½ cup plain flour
½ tsp baking powder
2 tbsp melted butter

Make ½ litre of milk, using milk powder and water, as per packet instructions, and keep aside, to use in making the dough. In a bowl, add 1 cup of the milk powder, plain flour, baking powder, and melted butter, mix to combine. Using the milk prepared earlier with the extra milk powder, add to the flour mixture and combine to make a soft dough. Mould small smooth round balls with the dough. In a deep frying pan or wok, heat some oil and fry the balls until golden brown in colour. Don't overcrowd the pan. The balls will sink to the bottom of the pan but will rise when cooked and will need to be turned to get an even shade of golden brown. The heat needs to be medium and not too hot. Using a slotted spoon, remove the balls onto absorbent paper to drain. Place the balls into the sugar syrup recipe below and leave to absorb the liquid for about 4 hours.

Serve in sugar syrup hot or cold.

Sugar Syrup
Serves 4/6

2 cups sugar
1 cup water
3-4 green cardamom pods, just broken open
A few strands of saffron

Place all the ingredients into a heavy bottomed saucepan and simmer over a gentle heat, making sure the sugar does not crystallize. This should take about 20 minutes. While the sugar syrup is warm, add the gulab jamuns to the syrup and leave to soak for a few hours.

Serve hot or cold.

Cornflake Sweets

Serves 4/6

2 cups cornflakes
1 cup roasted peanuts
1 tsp cardamom powder
1 cup jaggery, or sugar

In a wok, heat the jaggery with the cardamom powder until it has melted then heat for a further 1 minute. Add 1 tbsp of water if it is too thick. Take off the heat when cooked (the mixture will be extremely hot so be very careful). Stir the cornflakes and peanuts into mixture. Place paper cupcake cases onto a tray and drop a tablespoon of the mixture into each cupcake cases and leave to harden.

Serve.

Milk Cake

Serves 4/6

400g ricotta cheese
¼ cup semolina
½ cup sugar
1 tbsp sultanas or any dried fruit

Place all the ingredients into a bowl and mix to combine. Keep stirring for about 2 minutes to ensure all the ingredients have been incorporated. Pour the mixture into a greased loaf tin. Bake in the oven for 40 minutes at 180°C until browned all over. Remove by turning it out onto a plate and let it cool for 30 minutes, before cutting into squares.

Serve, the milk cake preferably warm, although it is good cold too.

Frozen Fruit Kebabs

Serves 4

Mixed fruit cut into chunks, such as strawberry, melon or kiwi fruit

Thread fruit onto pre-soaked bamboo skewers and place in the freezer for about 30 minutes.

Serve with fruit yoghurt.

Shrikhand with Pomegranate

Serves 4

500g thick Greek yoghurt (ensure it is thick and creamy)
1 cup sugar
Large pinch of saffron, soaked in 2 tbsp of milk
1 cup pomegranate seeds

In a bowl, beat the yoghurt with the sugar for about 5 minutes until the sugar has dissolved and the mixture is thick and creamy. Add the saffron and milk and give it another good stir. Pour into a 4 individual desert bowls and sprinkle with pomegranate seeds. Place the bowls in the fridge to cool.

Serve.

Ginger Ice Cream
Serves 4

1 litre vanilla ice cream
4 tsp ground ginger
Crystallized ginger for sprinkling

Take the ice cream out of the freezer and leave to soften at room temperature. Add the ground ginger to the ice cream and mix well. Place the ice cream back in ice cream container and sprinkle with crystallized ginger and freeze again.

Can be served with tamarind sauce (see below)

Tamarind Sauce
Serves 4

3 tbsp tamarind paste
25g brown sugar
20 dried dates, stones removed
¼ cup raisins

In a bowl, mix the dates and raisins with 250ml boiling water. Leave to soak for 30 minutes. Place the mixture into a blender with the sugar and tamarind paste and blend until smooth. Pour into a bowl and place in the fridge to cool.

Serve with ice cream.

Drinks

Masala Chai

Masala Chai is the most popular drink consumed in Indian households, and has now become popular all over the world. "Chai" is the Indian word for tea and masala is spice.

The traditional method for brewing tea is to infuse tea leaves with water, spice, milk and sugar. The spice is normally cardamoms, fennel or cinnamon. It is milky mixture.

There is not one single method for brewing tea, each individual household will have their own favourite version, and they all taste good.

Tea plants have grown in the Assam region of India, and were used in herbal medicine. It was only when the British East India Company were in India, and they wanted to end the monopoly of Tea from China that they noticed the tea plants in Assam they wanted to export tea to the UK where tea was very popular. The British East Company also introduced tea in mainstream India, but as with most foods the Indian people made it their own by adding spice to the tea. This was not what the Company had in mind, but masala Chai has grown in popularity, not only in India but the rest of the world.

Lassi

This is another popular drink and is a yoghurt based drink. It originated in the Punjab region of India and is blended yoghurt with water and sweetened with sugar or fruits or made savoury with salt. The salt version is the most popular in Punjab, even today.

Punch

Punch is drink popular all over the world, and is a mixture of fruit juices with or without alcohol.

The drink originated in India and it was the British East India Company who introduced the it back into England and then the rest of the world.

Punch is known as a loanword, from the Indian word in Hindi "Panch", which translates to Five, and the ingredients for the drink include, alcohol, water, lemon juice, sugar and spices.

Orange, Ginger and Mint Refresher
Serves 1

1 large glass of orange juice
½ tsp ginger powder
½ tsp ground mint extra for garnish

Place all the ingredients into a blender and blend until smooth. Sieve into a glass and enjoy with ice. Garnish with mint leaves.

Serve.

Masala Chai
Serves 2

4 cups water
1 tsp whole fennel seeds
6 green cardamom pods, ground
2 tea bags or 2 tsp of fresh tea leaves

Heat 4 cups water in a saucepan, add fennel seeds and cardamom. Bring to the boil, then lower the heat and simmer for 5 minutes to infuse the water with the spice flavours. Add the tea bags or fresh tea leaves and boil for a further 2 minutes. Add milk and sugar to taste and bring to the boil again. Remove from heat and sieve into cups.

Serve.

Ginger Tea
Serves 2

4 cups of water
1 tsp fresh ginger, finely sliced
2 tea bags
Milk and sugar to taste

Heat water in a saucepan, add ginger strands. Bring to the boil and continue boiling for at least 5 minutes. Add the tea bags and boil for a further 2 minutes. Sieve into a cup and add milk and sugar to taste.

Serve.

Cinnamon Hot Chocolate
Serves 2

4 cups whole milk
225g chocolate
3 tsp sugar
1 cinnamon stick

Chop chocolate into pieces and place in a saucepan with the milk, sugar and cinnamon stick. Heat and keep stirring so it does not stick to the bottom of the pan. Bring to boil then take off heat and whisk. Strain into cups and add a sprinkle of cinnamon on top.

Serve.

Chilli Hot Chocolate
Serves 2

½ cup whole milk
½ cup full cream
½ tsp cayenne pepper
150g good quality milk chocolate

In a saucepan, heat milk with cream and cayenne pepper. Bring to the boil, stirring all the time. Simmer gently for 3 to 4 minutes. Break the chocolate into small pieces and add to the milk and whisk. The cream and chocolate will take away some of the chilli spice.

Serve.

Lemonade and Mint
Serves 2

1 cup lime juice
1 tbsp lime zest
1 cup sugar
Handful of fresh mint leaves

In a saucepan, place 1 cup water, sugar and lime zest. Bring to the boil whilst stirring, to dissolve the sugar. Remove from heat and keep aside to cool. Once cool, strain into a jug and stir in lime juice with 2 cups of water. Add mint leaves to jug and serve cold over ice. If too sweet, add more lime juice.

Serve

Pink Lemonade
Serves 4

1 cup sugar
4 cups water
1 cup unsweetened cranberry juice
1 cup lemon juice

In a saucepan, heat sugar and 1 cup water. Bring to the boil, and whilst stirring dissolve the sugar, remove from heat and cool. Pour the syrup into a jug, stir in the remaining 3 cups of water, unsweetened cranberry juice and lemon juice. Chill in refrigerator for about 2 hours. Pour over ice. If using sweetened cranberry juice, reduce the amount of sugar used.

Serve garnished with mint leaves.

Mango Lassi
Serves 2

1 cup plain yoghurt
½ cup milk
1 mango, chopped
4 tsp sugar

In a blender, add the yoghurt, mango, milk and sugar. Blend for about 2 minutes until mango is pulped. Strain into individual glasses, and chill for 2 hours.

Serve garnished with mint leaves.
Optional: Try adding some cardamom powder to the mixture when blending or sprinkling some cardamom powder on top in the glass.

Ice Coffee
Serves 2

2 tsp instant coffee
4 tbsp warm water
A glass of ice cold milk
2 tsp sugar

In a small glass mix the instant coffee and sugar with warm water. Pour the ice cold milk into another glass and then add the instant coffee mixture. Mix with a spoon until combined. Add ice cubes.

Serve garnished with mint leaves.

Sweet Lassi
Serves 2

½ cup plain yoghurt
1 cup water
2 tsp sugar

In a blender, blend the yoghurt, water, sugar and rose water, if using for about 1 minute until a smooth consistency is achieved. Pour into a tall glass and chill for about 1 hour.

Serve garnished with mint leaves.
Optional: Add 1 tsp rose water.

Salt Lassi
Serves 2

½ cup plain yoghurt
1 cup water
1 tsp salt

In a blender, blend the yoghurt, salt and water for about 1 minute until a smooth consistency is achieved. Pour into a tall glass and chill.

Serve garnished with mint leaves.

Rose Ice Cream Shake
Serves 2

½ glass of milk
2 scoops of vanilla ice cream
1 tsp rose water

In a blender, add the milk, ice cream and rose water, and blend until smooth. Pour into tall glasses.

Serve.

Cola Ice Cream
Serves 2

½ glass cola
1 or 2 scoops of vanilla ice cream

Fill a glass with cola about two-thirds full. Add 1 to 2 scoops of ice cream.

Serve with a straw.

Spiced Coffee with Fennel and Cardamom
Serves 2

4 cups water
1 tsp whole fennel seeds
6 green cardamom pods, ground
1 tsp instant coffee

In a saucepan add the water, with the fennel and cardamom. Bring to boil and continue boiling for at least 5 minutes. Add coffee to a cup and sieve the boiled water over the coffee, stirring to combine. If preferred add milk and sugar to taste.

Serve.

Almond / Badam Milk
Serves 2

2 tsp plain flour
2 tsp melted butter
½ cup blanched almonds
2 cup milk

In a small saucepan, mix in butter and flour until it changes colour to golden brown, ensuring it does not burn. This should only take about 1 minute. Add the milk and keep stirring, then add the almonds. Add sugar to taste. Bring to boil and pour into a mug.

Serve.

Cold Milky Coffee
Serves 2

4 cups black instant coffee
1 cup cream
½ cup sugar
1 tsp vanilla extract

In a jug, add the freshly made black coffee with cream, sugar and vanilla extract. Stir and place in fridge to cool.

Serve in tall glasses garnished with mint leaves

Cumin Refresher with Mint
Serves 2

1 pack of fresh mint leaves
2 lemons juiced
pinch of salt
½ tsp cumin powder

Place all the ingredients into a blender and blend. Add a little water to form a smooth paste. Sieve the paste into a small jug. Discard the pulp. Place 1 tsp of juice into a tall glass and mix in water, carbonated water or lemonade and ice cubes.

Serve.

Strawberry Lassi
Serves 2

1 cup plain yoghurt
Handful of strawberries, frozen or fresh
2 tbsp sugar or to taste
½ cup milk

Place all the ingredients into a blender and blend until smooth. Pour into tall glasses and chill for about an hour.

Serve.
Optional: Add a couple of mint leaves as garnish.

Coconut Lassi

Serves 2

1 cup plain yoghurt
½ cup milk
2 tsp desiccated coconut
4 tsp sugar

In a blender, add the yoghurt, coconut, milk and sugar. Blend for about 2 minutes until mixture is smooth. Strain into individual glasses and chill for 2 hours.

Serve.

Optional: Try adding some cardamom powder to the mixture when blending or sprinkling some cardamom powder on top in the glasses.

Glossary of
Indian Spices
and Flavourings

India is the largest producer and exporter of spices and herbs around the globe, many of which are indigenous to India. To assist you in cooking Indian recipes, consult this list of spices and flavourings which gives both the Indian and English terms used for each item.

Not all of these spices have been used in this book and the list is not exhaustive, but it will help familiarise you with Indian spices, this will help you later when you experiment in adapting your own versions of Indian recipes.

Aamchur Powder	Mango Powder	A tart flavor
Ajwain	Carom Seeds	
Anardana	Pomegranate Seeds	
Anardana Powder	Pomegranate Powder	A tart flavor
Adrak	Ginger	
Choti Elaichi	Green Cardamom	Native to Kerala
Badi Elaichi / Kali Elaichi	Black Cardamom	
Dalchini	Cinnamon	Grown to Kerala
Dhania	Whole Coriander Seeds	
Pisa Dhania	Coriander Powder	
Hari Dhania	Green Coriander Leaves	
Garam Masala	A number of spices blended together	Different brands will contain different spices and quantities

Gulab Jal	Rose Water	Used in desserts
Gur / Jaggery	Unrefined Sugar	Made with the sap of sugarcane. Native to North India
Haldi	Turmeric	Imparts the yellow colour in recipes
Hari Mirch	Whole Green Chilli	Used whole or chopped; the smaller in size the hotter they will be as a general rule
Lal Mirch	Whole Red Chilli or Red Chilli Powder	These can be used whole or chopped. Not as hot as the green chillies, and often found dried. The red chilli powder can be used in place of chilli flakes
Hing	Asafoetida	Optional to use in Indian cooking, but we have not used this spice in this book. If used, only a very small amount is required. It has a sulphur smell uncooked, but when cooked there is no smell, and used to aid digestion
Imli	Tamarind	A tart flavor, used in sauces and chutneys
Jeera	Cumin Seeds	Used whole or in powder form
Kala Namak	Black Salt	May have a slight sulphur smell
Kali Mirchi	Black Pepper	Largest export from Kerala

Kalonji	Onion Seeds / Nigella Seeds	
Kasoori Methi	Dried Fenugreek Leaves	
Kesar	Saffron	Known as the world's most expensive Spice. The best saffron comes from Kashmir in India
Khus Khus	Poppy Seeds	
Lahsun	Garlic	
Lavang	Cloves	
Methi	Fenugreek	Used as seeds or fresh leaves
Namak / Nool	Salt	
Nimbu	Lemon / Limes	
Pudina	Mint	
Pyaz	Onions	
Panch Phoran	A blend of 5 spices	Widely used in Guajarati cooking, containing a blend of 5 powdered spices in equal quantities: cumin, fenugreek, mustard, kalonji and aniseed
Rai	Brown Mustard Seeds	

Saunf	Fennel Seeds	
Sirka	Vinegar	
Tej Patta	Bay Leaf	
Sambar Powder	Spice Blend of different spices	Mostly used in South Indian cooking
Chaat Masala	Spice Blend of different spices	Tangy and used sprinkled over dishes

Glossary of
Indian Terms

Achar	Indian Pickle
Am	Mango
Aloo Tikki	Aloo = Potato Tikki = Patty
Atta	Chapati Flour
Badam	Almonds
Besan	Chickpea Flour
Bhuna	A cooking process, where spices are cooked in oil and the resulting dish is dry with no gravy
Barfi	Indian Sweet
Bhutra	A type of deep fried bread
Boondi	Little round balls made with chickpea flour and usually served in yoghurt to form a raita
Chapati / Roti	Indian Bread
Cholay / Channa	Whole Chickpeas
Dosa	Crepe-like rolled pancakes normally stuffed with potato mixture and served with a tangy lentils
Gobi Aloo	Gobi = Cauliflower Aloo = Potato
Gulab Jamun	Indian dessert or sweet made of round balls soaked in sugar syrup

Gur / Jaggery	Unrefined and concentrated cane juice sugar can be golden brown or dark brown in colour
Halva	Indian Dessert
Jelbi	Indian sweets usually bright yellow in colour and soaked in sugar syrup
Kitchri	A dish made with Rice and Lentils
Kheer	Indian Rice Pudding
Kulfi	Indian Ice Cream
Kaju	Cashew Nuts
Khajur	Dates
Kish Mish	Raisins
Ladoo	An Indian sweet shaped in round balls
Lassi	Indian Drink made with Yoghurt
Maki di Roti	Bread made with Chickpea flour
Methi	Fenugreek Leaves, fresh or dried, otherwise known as Katsuri Methi
Okra / Ladies Finger	Green vegetable, texture gets slimy when wet
Pakoras	An Indian snack of deep fried vegetables in Chickpea flour
Paneer	Indian Cheese, similar to Cottage Cheese

Papdi	Crisp-like discs made with flour normally served in the Bel Puri dish
Paratha	Indian Bread can be filled with different ingredients
Peshwari	Naan Bread filled with nuts and fruit such as raisins, coconut or pistachios
Pomfret	A fish found in the Indian Ocean and a specialty of South India. Substitute with any white fish.
Poori	Deep fried Indian Bread made with Chapati flour
Rasamali	Indian Dessert
Saag	A dish made with Spinach
Sambal	A spicy condiment normally served with Dosas
Sandesh	Indian Dessert
Sarson	Mustard Green Leaves native to Punjab region of India and used to make Saag
Sarson Tel	Sarson = Mustard Tel = Oil Mustard Oil
Sev	Long thin and crisp strands made with flour; forms part of Indian Bombay mix or used in Belpuri
Shimla Mirchi	Peppers or Capsicums
Shrikhand	Indian Dessert

Index

Snacks and Starters

Potato Crisps	21
Potato Pakoras	10
Potato Wedges	18
Prawns in Breadcrumbs	17
Prawn Pakoras	17
Salt and Chilli Almonds	18
Spicy Corn on the Cob	26
Spicy Jacket Potato	31
Spicy Popcorn	15
Spicy Potato Chapati Wrap	25
Stuffed Sweet Peppers	16
Sweet and Chilli Biscuits	19
Sweet Eggy Bread	7
Tandoori Pizza	27
Tandoori Chicken Chapati Wrap	24
Tangy Chips	15
Tomatoes on Toast	8
Tomato and Chilli Penne Pasta	9
Tuna and Chilli Angel Hair Pasta	29
Vegetable Samosas	11
Zucchini Flowers filled with Paneer	21

Meals

Beef

Beef with Chilli Butter	69
Chilli Steak	68
Crumbed Beef with Chilli Butter	69
Indian Beef Burgers	68
Minced Beef Pie	65
Spicy Fillet Steak	67
Spicy Steak	65
Steak with Orange Marinade	66
Steak with Chilli Sauce	66
Steak with Pomegranate	64
Tamarind Chilli Beef	67

Chicken

Lamb

Pork

Seafood

Vegetarian

Marinades and Paste

Indian Curries

Dhal / Lentils

Saag

Drinks

Web Site

Please take the time to have to have a look at the web site **www.indiancookingfouringredients.com** which accompanies this book. It contains more recipes, insights to Indian cooking, new ideas and where to buy spices.

Indian cooking does not have to be time consuming and with so many new spice combinations available, it is so easy to create wonderful menus to please all tastes.

The web site is updated often with new information.

Notes

INDIAN COOKING WITH FOUR INGREDIENTS

Notes

Notes

INDIAN COOKING WITH FOUR INGREDIENTS

Notes

Notes

INDIAN COOKING WITH FOUR INGREDIENTS